The Emancipation Of

Tithing

Discovering Your Freedom
From
Financial Slavery

M. D. Ewing

The Emancipation
Of

Tithing

Discovering Your Freedom
From
Financial Slavery

By

M. D. Ewing

The Emancipation of Tithing
Discovering Your Freedom From Financial Slavery

Unless otherwise indicated, all Scripture quotations are taken from the Holy Bible, New Living Translation, copyright © 1996, 2004, 2007 by Tyndale House Foundation. Used by the permission of Tyndale House Publishers, Inc., Carol Stream, Illinois 60188. All rights reserved.

ISBN 978-0-9855490-0-8

Published By:

Enlightenment Publishing, LLC

P.O. Box 480442

New Haven, MI 48048

enlightpub@gmail.com

Contents Within The Book

The Author's Corner

Who is the author? It has always been the proper protocol to introduce yourself to your potential audience in the form of biography–permitting viewers to get a glimpse of your life's history. My name is Mitchell D. Ewing and I am the husband to my beautiful wife Bridget, and we share the love of our four beautiful children: Zaria, Zanetta, Zashanae, and Mitchell Jr. I was born in Detroit, Michigan, but later resided in Suffolk, Virginia, due to my enlistment into the military. Virginia is where I came to know Christ and became a student of the gospel well over 22 years ago. I've been graced to obtain three degrees, one being a Master of Business Administration. I desire to pursue my doctorate in psychology and will obtain it when time grants me the opportunity to achieve it. So who is the author? I am a man who loves Christ as well as his wife and family. I am a man who enjoys the simpler things in life. I am a man who grew up in poverty, but now understands that education is the prosperity of the mind.

It is not necessarily in the number of degrees you possess, but in the freedom of obtaining knowledge and the liberty of gaining understanding, learning something new each day that was hidden from you in years past. Knowledge endorses power, but there will be many who would keep you powerless in ignorance. I truly enjoy learning from people with sound material and sharing that knowledge with others. I enjoy talking to people about things that matter most to them–things that can positively impact a person's physical, spiritual, mental, and emotional well-being. For these four attributes are what defines human nature and are a resume of your current state of being. If one of these characteristics is damaged then the others will soon be negatively impacted. That's why it is extremely important to seek help from those who specialize in restoring health to any of your distinguishing traits. Furthermore, I believe that it is remarkably important that every man and woman live with a sense of freedom–meaning that no one should live their life under the manipulation, control, and bondage of another person, based on fear, terror, or intimidation. I am not speaking as if I arrived to a certain echelon of human nature, being a complete human being, but I have come to a place in my own life where I am not afraid to acknowledge my inadequacies, nor am I afraid to ask for assistance. Neither am I afraid to challenge the majority, especially when I have thoroughly researched a subject based on facts and history, even if I appear to be the minority. I can truly say that I enjoy being me, to include all areas of my strengths and weaknesses. Furthermore, I truly enjoy living and being free–free in mind and body, free in spirit and soul.

The Emancipation of Tithing

Thanks
and Dedication

I would simply like to thank God for his love and care for my soul, mind, and body, for it was he who saved me from self-destruction. I would also like to thank my beautiful wife and children for supporting me continuously. To my father, mother, and my wonderful sisters, I say thank you. To my true friends who have been reliable in friendship, prayer, and love, for both my family, and me I say thank you and let's continue striving together in friendship. To all who read this book and gain a new point of view on tithing, may God be with you on your new journey–and a special thanks to you. I dedicate this book to every person who is willing to gain a new perspective on this past practice of giving–making significant changes. It is not easy to adjust to new things, especially when you have been repeating a practice for many years. But I always tell myself concerning change, "to know something and not implement it is the same as never knowing it at all." Why take the time to learn something, get excited about it, and then remain in the same state as before. I know firsthand the mindset of an individual who has to make a choice between being free or being confronted with ridicule, or remaining in bondage and being well-liked by both family and friends.

I also know the challenge of accepting this financial freedom, even though the majority of people would say different, oftentimes making you feel like an outcast. It's a tough place, but remaining spiritually detained is not a comfortable place either. But when it is all said and done, you have to trust God; it was God through Christ who saved and comforted me. Before the establishment of your church or ministry, before the calling of your pastors and leaders, before the connecting of your family and friends, it has always been God and it will always be

God when those people, places, and things are no longer available to meet your requirements. It takes Godly courage to make unpopular choices, and boldness to stand for something when no one else will. I pray that as you read this book, that through the Scriptures you gain more courage and boldness toward your financial freedom and become emancipated from the slavery of tithing.

Introduction

This book was written to give everyone the opportunity to understand the past and present practices of this ancient tradition, giving every reader the knowledge and an alternative view to the practices of today. For those who can, please keep an open heart and mind to view these passages of Scripture outside what you have already preconceived as truth. Before we begin this exciting topic, I would like to enlighten you about a practice that is often overlooked when it comes down to the Bible and the interpretation of the Scriptures. This practice is referred to as "hermeneutics," which is the art and science of biblical interpretation.

The most important lesson for properly interpreting the Bible and the Scriptures relating to each passage is based on how well we understand the surrounding context of the story being portrayed. Do we understand all the facts in each passage? Do we understand the context before and after each passage? Have we biblically defined the meanings of all the words surrounding each passage? How well do we understand the general flow of discussion? Do we have an indication of the cultural background at hand? What did the author mean in the day that he/she wrote the passage? It is imperative that we clear up all the factual problems before moving into the theological meaning of any passage of Scripture. It is also important to visualize yourself as a participant in the crowd of the original audience in order to understand the authenticity of the original message.

There are two terms that are always used when practicing the art of hermeneutics. The first term is known as, "eisegesis" (ice-sa-ge-sis), which means to read your own meaning into a passage. Interpreting the Bible correctly begins with a great deal of prayer, learning how to pay attention to what the text itself is saying, and then pulling the meaning out of each passage. This term is called, "exegesis" (ex-sa-ge-sis), which means to draw out from. We must allow each passage to be defined by what is actually in the text of Scriptures, supported by the surrounding verses of the text, if we intend on interpreting the Bible in context and in a correct manner. We can no longer put into a passage of Scripture our own meanings and interpretations about a particular subject when that subject is not listed or included in the passage at hand. This is called "bias demeanor" and "subjectivity," which is the framework of silent manipulation and control.

For example, if I said, "Farmers sow seeds in the ground to bring up a harvest," this text should NOT be interpreted as, "People should give me money in order to gain possessions." This is a primary example of bias demeanor and subjectivity. As the author of that statement, I literally meant what I stated, that farmers who plant seeds in the ground will grow a harvest. As you see, my original message can easily be misinterpreted if the meanings of all the words surrounding the context are misunderstood, and if the meaning of the original writer is misunderstood then the true meaning behind the story could be lost forever.

It has always been my desire to educate many on the subject of tithing, giving everyone the freedom and opportunity to understand the purposes of tithing in the proper context, rather than the bias demeanor and subjectivity of many teachings. We will examine every aspect of tithing from the history of the practice and beyond. I must admit the tithing practices of today do not reflect the original practices of old biblical history. One of the main focuses of the tithe (from the original practices of old biblical history) and the tither was to care for those less fortunate (on which we will focus more in depth later in the book). Can you say that the tithes you see collected in your church, ministry, temple, synagogue, etc., are being used more for personal needs/personal projects rather than the needs/desires of other people? Don't be misled. What you are observing is what it actually is.

Let me set the tone by asking you this question: Have you personally ever done a biblical study on tithing? Have you personally ever actually observed the Scriptures on tithing outside of how it's preached or taught (by the means of many adding their own meanings into the passages even before observing the surrounding context of Scriptures and the defining of words)? Are you (as I was) caught up in the hype of paying God his due or else you'll be cursed with a curse by God; and, on the other end of that teaching, you were often made to pay your tithes if you wanted God to open up the windows of heaven and pour you out a blessing that there shall not be room enough for you to receive. (This teaching will be discussed later on in the book.)

Even to the point of you giving up your rent money or the money that was needed for you to pay bills or buy groceries. I know that if you're reading this right now many of you stand victimized or guilty of not paying your taxes for the sake of paying tithes. Going broke, hungry, bill collectors calling you, rent due, and all you can say to the collectors is, "I paid my tithes and God is going to get his first." Is that really what tithing was all about in the Old Testament? Is that really what God designed the tithing system of old to do? Did God allow the tithing system under the Levitical priesthood as a pattern for us today to become bad stewards and bad examples of his love and power by being broke while waiting on a promise that is greatly misinterpreted, and the only hope you have left is to lean on what is often said, "Your ship of blessings is about to dock or is coming in."

I challenge you today, brothers and sisters in Christ, leaders of all races, creeds, colors, and religions who practice tithing, to examine this topic closely with me as we discover the true practices behind tithing. As we approach the beginning of this important topic, we will draw from what is in the passages of Scriptures and not put our own meanings into it. This subject topic is very controversial because our consciences have been constrained so much and for so long by this doctrine of tithing that when God blesses us we think it's because of the tithes we paid over the many years, and when something bad happens to us, we say that it's God cursing us because we failed to pay our tithes. If the car breaks down, if the refrigerator stops working, if the fuses in our homes or apartments go bad, we are taught that we are to blame for these things happening because we have not been paying our tithes. If we have been paying tithes, we then blame it on ourselves for not being good stewards of our finances.

My brothers and sisters, have you ever noticed that even while you were paying tithes these things still happened to you? Why? Because everything that has been made by and through mankind is temporal, incomplete, and cannot last forever. Things are guaranteed to fail, go bad, or need replacing. Have you ever heard in this life of an automobile being made and never having problems, never needing maintenance or new parts, never having to be replaced or upgraded? Why then when something natural, like a car breaking down on us, is it automatically linked to us not paying our tithes. I know why, because it's from the years of our minds being mesmerized by a teaching that we have recreated for the purpose of self-gratification and as a requirement for membership (in some churches as a part of your salvation) in today's churches.

Oftentimes many leaders use clichés (clever sayings) to help support their beliefs on tithing, either by using

Scriptures out of the proper context with carnal reasoning, or by using no biblical references at all. How do many use it out of context? I'll give you a few examples: We will go to all of the Scriptures in the New Testament that address general "giving," and then we'll change the thought pattern from "giving" to "tithing," when the Scriptures were only addressing "freewill" giving. We'll show you many Scriptures about "sowing seed" and then address the seed sown as being money. Please understand that there are more biblical passages that reference "the seed" as being a male's semen than reference of "the seed" as being money. Go back and research. The Bible rarely addresses "seed" as being money, in comparison to the vast teachings of the term, which 99% of the time is in reference to money rather than the true definition defined in each passage. Where do we derive this concept that every time the word "seed" in Scriptures appears we often relate that text to mean "money"? Maybe it is because that teaching has been what our minds, over many years, have been conditioned to think. It is a recognized and proven fact that many of us never really took the time to study the doctrine of tithing (though we were, and some still are, dedicated tithers). And why should we take the time to study this topic when there is no way that the preacher, teacher, pastor, or leader would ever lie to us? In some cases, yes, they are human and capable of making mistakes, but many of them never really took the time to examine this topic themselves-because the money that's coming into the organization, church, ministry, etc., is pretty good.

Here are examples of clever and convincing clichés:

"Tithing was a form of worship to God, and since we still worship God, we must still tithe." Well, this could also be said: "Since the burning of animals was a form of worshiping God, and since we still worship God, we should still be required to offer the burning of animals to God."

"Jesus Christ is the same yesterday, today, and forever, and God never changes so tithing never changes." Once again, in that case, this can also be said: "Since Jesus Christ is the same yesterday, today, and forever, and God never changes, we must continue to stone people to death when they break one of God's commandments."

Over the course of time, I had heard so many nonbiblical clichés on tithing that I believed I had heard them all–that was, until I heard these:

- Tithing is like paying rent to God.

- Tithing is like paying and keeping your insurance premiums paid up in case things go bad.

- Tithing is putting your money in God's heavenly account, stored up for hard times.

- Tithing is a link between God and your blessings.

- By tithing -- your children's children will be blessed

What does that statement imply? Does it indicate that when my children and my children's children are older - they will not be required to tithe because they are blessed through my tithing? No, that's not what it suggests because everyone is obligated to tithe. So then, what is the meaning of this proverb, which is often quoted, but not biblically confirmed? Jesus stated, in what we refer to as the "Beatitudes" found in the book of Matthew 5:1-12,

"God blesses those who are poor and realize their need for him, for the Kingdom of Heaven is theirs.

God blesses those who mourn, for they will be comforted.

God blesses those who are humble, for they will inherit the whole earth.

God blesses those who hunger and thirst for justice, for they will be satisfied...."

However, you will NOT find anywhere Jesus stating or God implying, **"Blessed are they that tithe, for their children's children will be blessed."**

I will show you where this concept is derived from later in the book.

- The blessing on Abraham's life was because of the tithing covenant he made with God.

Did Abraham make a tithing covenant with God? We will revisit this idea later on in the subject topic "Tithing Before the Law."

Over the course of many years, we as Christians have received all of these chronicles, witty sayings, and many others in our consciences without ever really challenging the authenticity of the Scriptures that should follow these creative opinions. The truth is, there are no scriptural backings to follow many of the self-defined/imposed teachings we hear today. Why are so many Christian families today of all races (to include those in the African American communities) struggling financially, or are poor, and the only ones who seem to be prospering are the church leaders? I am not against leaders who prosper, absolutely not; but why do they have to flourish financially on our account or get rich at the expense of God's hardworking people?

Why do I have to believe in God by faith to thrive economically, according to the Word of God, and my leader doesn't need to trust God or need faith to financially prosper? He/she just uses our tithes and offerings as their main source of income (over and above

10%). What they receive is not by faith, it's all stationary. Faith is not stationary. They strategically calculate their pay (using the governmental, church, and law percentages and not using common sense based on the needs of the church); they analyze their raises, and they adopt a lifestyle of living in luxury, which is not by faith but by their stationary rewards that come in the form of tithes, offerings, birthdays, anniversaries, and let me not forget, the people who are taught to sow into the men/women of God's life in order to receive a blessing. After exhausting people's income, these leaders use the money to start their own businesses (i.e., write books, open productive companies, make movies,) involving themselves in financial kickbacks to continue their luxurious living. So if asked, "How did you obtain all of this wealth?" they can answer, I wrote books..., my own business... and so on. But the source of their income, prior to involving themselves in these financial kickbacks (which is ingenious) still came from God's people's money. Yes, there are those who will say or boast about the amount of money they were making prior to accepting the office of a pastor, teacher, evangelist, or any other leadership position: however, what they were making prior to accepting the office, in comparison, is like a dime to every dollar. So when God's people are taught, "You can have what I have…if you only give and have faith," how can that be when it didn't take faith to gain their own wealth?

I speak as one who has witnessed many of these accounts from the inside out and not the outside in. In other words, many people will never have the opportunity to witness these meetings, events, conversations, etc., that take place behind closed doors with many of their own leaders, more than just on Sunday mornings. I'm not writing this book to expose their personal faults and failures, but I am writing this book to give many a different view of this important topic and to expose this common practice, to encourage people to make better decisions when handling their own income that God has provided them.

Let me interject and express this thought: Many leaders possibly will make the statement that they are faithful tithers, but are they really tithers? Yes, they do indeed pay tithes, but many of them get that same tithe money recycled to them by the end of the week in the form of their paychecks received from the church. When you tithe, do you get that same tithed money recycled to your paycheck at the end of the week? I mean, do you really consider that a tithe? How about encouraging your leaders to take the money that they set aside as tithes and instead of putting it in the church's money tray, encourage them to give their tithes to a smaller or less income-based ministry or charity that has no involvement with your ministry (on a continual basis). Now that's a real tithe according to today's practices. Just a thought! Let me continue!

This is one of phases most often used, "Blessings flow from the head down," (meaning if the clergyman or woman gets rich, you'll get rich by following them), and then Psalms 133 is used, which is not "biblically based"; this chapter of Scripture relates totally to "unity". The unity of the brothers/sisters dwelling together, the unity of the ointment that flowed down Aaron's beard, and when it flowed down, the ointment was still together, and when it flowed down to Aaron's skirt, the ointment was still together. In unity is where God's blessing flows, not your men or women of God. (Search it out.) All leaders do not operate in this fashion; however, many of them do. If you'll be still and observe long enough, God will reveal the truth of his Word through what you observe. Now that bothers leaders when people are told to observe what's being preached/taught from the pulpit; however, let me call to your attention this passage of Scripture:

Acts 17:10-11

"That very night the believers sent Paul and Silas to Berea. When they arrived there, they went to the Jewish Synagogue.

And the people of Berea were more opened minded than those in Thessalonica, and they listened eagerly to Paul's message. They searched the Scriptures day after day to see if Paul and Silas were preaching the truth."

The word "searching" in this passage of Scripture comes from the Greek meaning to examine or judge, to enquire into, to scrutinize, to sift, and to question as in an investigation or interrogation sense. Some leaders will tell you by doing this, you will become critical of the Scriptures; however, according to this definition and passage of Scripture, it is our duty to do this if we would like to become wise and be considered noble like those in the city of Berea. Start investigating what you're being taught; it is not a sin to do so. Jesus even stated in the book of:

St. John 5:39

"You search the Scriptures because you think they give you eternal life. But the Scriptures point to me!"

Studying the Scriptures doesn't make you critical of somebody else's preaching; studying the Scriptures allows you to see Christ in the midst of all these strange and perverse doctrines and teachings. When the apostle Paul addressed the church in the book of Ephesians 4:14, he stated that we as a people should come to a point in our lives that we grow in faith and in the knowledge of Christ, becoming mature in the Lord so that we should no longer be immature, like kids convinced and manipulated by every new thought or teaching. He also expressed to the church not to allow the influence of those people who may be esteemed as important, to trick them with convincing sayings and lies about things that sound like or could be perceived as truth.

A lot of leaders use several passages from Old Testament Scriptures out of context and share them with their congregations as the foundation or a command from God on how you should take care of the leaders in your organization. In the book of I Kings 17:1-13, this text pertains to the widow woman making the prophet a cake before she and her son die; however, God sustains them. Please also note in verse 9 of this passage that God told the prophet that he has "already commanded" a widow woman to take care of him as he moves to the destination to which God commanded the prophet to go. If God already predestined this widow woman to feed the prophet, what is it that the prophet did that was so miraculous of his own accord? In the book of II Kings 4:1-7, this text pertains to a widow woman whose husband left an enormous amount of debt behind. The prophet gave her instructions on how to maintain her sons and possessions. This is true that God had given the prophet the wisdom to inspire this widow to survive; however, the prophet doesn't charge her for his words that were spoken, neither did he set up payment plans or ask her to sow into his life on a continuous basis. In the book of II Kings 5:1-14, this text pertains to Naaman, the captain of the host of the King of Syria, and how he was healed of leprosy by God through the prophet. This particular prophet refused to take financial gain from Naaman, because the prophet would not take the credit for what God had done. When the prophet's servant went in secret to collect financial gain from Naaman, he was cursed with leprosy.

In every one of these examples, when you read the full story, these were one-time instances where God used prophets with purposes for His glory and for the sake of healing and blessing others. These exact occurrences were never repeated. Though people were healed from similar diseases and blessed, these exact occurrences and particular situations were never repeated, which means these are NOT principles for us to practice today.

Principles can be defined as a quality of characteristics accepted or professed as a repeated rule of action or conduct. When something is practiced, it brings about a constant pattern of repetition. If something is done once, maybe twice, then those should be considered as single or double occurrences and not practices/principles. Furthermore, in these instances none of these prophets were filthy rich, nor do you see any of the many prophets throughout the entire Bible having the same occurrences where people had to sow in the prophet's life for his own personal gain. Finally, neither do you see God establishing these examples as the foundation for Christians today in which we should sow into the lives of our pastors/leaders in order to be blessed. We are blessed because of HIM and not them. If you do so, let it be done because you want it to be a blessing from your own heart and not manipulated by these Scripture passages.

I believe that there are benefits suitable for a person who preaches the gospel of Christ for a living; benefits that are freely offered in appreciation and respect to the office. However, I do not believe that anyone who is called to preach the gospel should demand, influence, or obligate you to financially be responsible for providing all of their personal necessities and desires as a direct commandment of God. Christ and many other leaders of the gospel were all privileged to receive food, clothing, and shelter at times, but you'll never see where any biblical preacher of the gospel became filthy rich by serving in the office.

Introduction

The apostle Paul expressed to the church at Corinth (I Corinthians 9:14) that it is only right for those who labor in the preaching the gospel of Christ (as their livelihood) should be supported by those who benefit from it. In addition, Paul continues to express that he never used any of these rights but would rather die than to lose the right to boast about the fact that he preached the gospel without cost and without price. So the question I have is this: Does Christ require his people to make his leaders rich? If so, Paul was disobedient because he never followed that commandment and was never made filthy rich. If Christ did not as a commandment obligate the general population of Christians to meet every imaginable craving for his leaders then why teach it as an obligation in today's society? If you have a yearning to learn, then you will love and enjoy this book. However, I do understand that many still will not believe or accept this teaching no matter what they see, read, or discover because they have believed for years that they are blessed based on their tithes and not because of their salvation and the fact that they are God's seed.

We will explore true giving and its purposes for our generation today.

Introduction

CHAPTER ONE

TITHING BEFORE
THE LAW

I discovered throughout biblical history that the practice of giving 10%, or the custom of paying tithes, was an ancient ritual found among many nations of the prehistoric world. The practice of giving a tithe extends into Hebrew history before the time of the Mosaic Law. There are only a few passages/instances recorded in the Bible that talk about someone tithing or demonstrating a vow to pay tithes before tithing was instituted in the law.

Oftentimes people use these passages out of context to prove to you why it is right to tithe. "Because it was before the law," and that's true. It was before the law; however, what does it truly mean for tithing to be instituted before the law? Let's define the word "law" because this word will play a very important part throughout this chapter. The Hebrew and Greek meaning of the word "law" is defined as rules, instructions, customs, commands, manners, requirements, injunctions, and legal directives. So, according to the definition of the word "law," if tithing was before the law, which it was, then by definition we can say that there were **no** commands, **no** rules, **no** precepts, **no** customs, **no** legal directives **nor** requirements that these tithes were to be paid or promised.

The phrase "tithing before the law" is often used to support why tithes should be required in our giving today; however, by definition, that phrase supports "tithing having no legal requirements" or "tithing before the requirements," which is the same statement as "tithing before the law." In the book of Genesis 14,

Melchizedek never asked Abraham to pay tithes, nor did he command him (Abraham) to do so.

As stated earlier, the practices of tithing were often used by many nations as a way to pay homage and respect to the office of priests as representatives of God, or to the gods themselves. In those days, "the tenth" was also referred to as the "heap" or the "topmost pick." This practice was used often during war between nations; the winner of the battle collected the riches taken from the enemy they defeated. As an offering to their gods for the victory of war, the best treasures (recovered) were gathered and placed at the top of all that was collected and a heap was taken from the top and offered to the priests or the gods of that nation, then the remainder of the treasure was given to the kings, then divided among warriors who participated in the fight.

This holds true in biblical history because in this context of Scripture in Genesis 14, Abraham practiced this same way of giving. Who told/taught Abraham to offer a tithe to the priest? Where did he get this ideal from, honoring a representative of God? In these passages of Scriptures, one thing that we can say from

Tithing Before the Law

what we read is that Melchizedek never commanded Abraham (his prior name being Abram) to offer anything. We must remember in the book of:

Joshua 24:2

"Joshua said to the people, this is what the Lord, the God of Israel, says: Long ago your ancestors, including Terah, the father of Abraham and Nahor, lived beyond the Euphrates River, and they worshiped other gods."

We forget that Abraham didn't always follow and serve the God of heaven and earth and that he had practices and rituals prior to being called by God. What practices and rituals did Abraham do prior to following the God of heaven and earth? We may never know the exact things that he practiced, but we can say that Abraham had cultural differences prior to being called by the God of heaven and earth. In the book of Genesis 14, Abraham had heard that his nephew Lot was taken as a prisoner; and, when he had heard this, Abraham, along with the men of his household, who were well-equipped in the art of war, went to rescue Lot. After rescuing his nephew Lot, Abraham brought back with him all the material goods that he obtained in battle. However, some of the material goods that Abraham possessed belonged to a king by the name of Sodom.

Now I would like to make an interesting point for you to see. As Abraham went to liberate Lot, he not only rescued Lot and his personal possessions, but all the possessions that were taken by these other nations, of which some (that were recovered) were owned by the King of Sodom. In Genesis 14:17, Abraham was returning from war and was planning to meet with the King of Sodom in a location that is referred to as the "King's Valley". Why? Because the passage of Scriptures informs us that Abraham was planning to return to the King of Sodom all of his personal possessions that he recovered from war. But, while he was waiting in the King's Valley for the King of Sodom, Abraham met King Melchizedek, who was also in the King's Valley simultaneously with Abraham. When Abraham met Melchizedek, who was also referred to as a priest, the passage of Scriptures tells us that he blessed Abraham and told him that he was highly favored of God and acknowledged that God had given Abraham the ability to be victorious over his enemies during battle. Then something unique happens. The passage of information goes on to say that Abraham gave Melchizedek a tenth of the spoils recovered from war.

What inspired Abraham to give a tenth of the spoils? It wasn't asked for nor required. So why did he do it, could it be from his prior practices and rituals before following the God of heaven and earth? What we can say is that he had just won a war and taken back spoils. Notice, according to what's written, before Abraham gave Melchizedek any tithes, Melchizedek blessed Abraham and called him blessed. Why? Because God had already declared Abraham blessed.

Genesis 12:1-3

"The LORD had said to Abram, 'Leave your native country, your relatives, and your father's family, and go to the land that I will show you.

I will make you into a great nation. I will bless you and make you famous, and you will be a blessing to others.

I will bless those who bless you and curse those who treat you with contempt. All the families on earth will be blessed through you. "

This covenant that God made with Abraham at this particular setting in the scriptural passage was not based on a "tithing covenant" as I hear many preach and teach, but it was made on Abraham believing (by faith) in what God had promised him and by Abraham demonstrating his belief by leaving (those things that were familiar to him) his country, people, and family behind to follow God (an unfamiliar voice). The book of Romans 4:13, reminds us that the promise made to Abraham that he should be great, successful and be made a great nation did not come by observing the commands of the law, but through the righteousness of his faith. The promise to Abraham was not based on observing any laws (because the Mosaic laws were not established yet), which means it wasn't the tithes that made Abraham blessed, it was God's purpose and promises declared on his life that made him blessed. In Genesis 12, you will notice that King Pharaoh blessed Abraham with riches.

In Genesis 13, the Bible says that Abraham became very rich and you do not see where Abraham sought for Melchizedek to pay tithes. Why, because there were no requirements to pay tithes before the law. The whole

Tithing Before the Law

purpose of why Abraham was in the Kings Valley was to return to the King of Sodom his material goods that were recovered from war. When the King of Sodom finally met up with Abraham, he told Abraham that he could keep all of his material goods, but required Abraham to return to him his people. However, Abraham refused to take anything from the King of Sodom, stating that he didn't want the King of Sodom to go around boasting that he had made him rich. Because the riches that Abraham had already acquired came from other sources, such as Pharaoh and Abimelech. These two kings had made Abraham rich. Furthermore, Abraham stated to Sodom that he had taken nothing for himself except the things that his men had **eaten** to sustain them during battle, encouraging those men with him to take their portion of the goods.

Abraham eventually returned all the goods to the King of Sodom that were recovered from war (except the food that was eaten by those involved in war). Though God used Pharaoh and Abimelech to make Abraham rich, Abraham didn't want to be associated with the King of Sodom in making him even richer. But I would like to pose a question to you? What did Abraham pay tithes

Tithing Before the Law

from? Well, according to **Genesis 14:20 and Hebrews 7:4:**

Genesis 14:20

"And blessed be God Most High, who has defeated your enemies for you. Then Abram gave Melchizedek a tenth of all the goods he had recovered."

Hebrews 7:4

"Consider then how great this Melchizedek was. Even Abraham, the great patriarch of Israel, recognized this by giving him a tenth of what he had taken in battle."

Now this is going to mess with your theology. The passage of Scriptures says that Abraham paid tithes from the spoils he recovered from battle. In other words, Abraham paid tithes from someone else's goods (these goods included food, not just possessions). Abraham paid tithes from the spoils he recovered from war, not from his own substance received from Pharaoh and Abimelech, but from the spoils received from war (according to what is written in biblical history). Remember, Abraham confessed in Genesis 14 to the King of Sodom that he had not (personally) taken any of his goods, except the things that his men used to eat and for their purposes. Abraham swore to the God of heaven on that statement that he made in Genesis 14:22-24. That was true–Abraham had not taken anything for himself that he recovered from war; however, he did give to Melchizedek (the priest) a tithe from someone else's resources.

Metaphorically speaking, that is equivalent to going into your pastor's personal bank account and drawing out $100,000, then paying 10% to a different church located in the same community, then returning to the pastor the remainder of his/her money. Sounds naïve; however, that is very similar to what had taken place in Abraham's day. Furthermore, I could respond to the pastor from whom the $100,000 was withdrawn by telling him/her that I had not taken any money for myself, and that would be a true statement. The fact remains that Abraham paid a tithe (from someone else's spoils) to Melchizedek. Even though he received material wealth from Pharaoh and Abimelech, it's not recorded anywhere that Abraham paid tithes from his own assets. We cannot assume that he did, because it is not written. There is nothing stated in those passages of Scripture that would cause us to conclude that Abraham ever tithed on a regular basis on his own personal possessions. As we have been taught earlier, to assume that Abraham paid tithes on a regular basis would be adding our own meaning and interpretation into the Scriptures; and, many will do that to support their own personal interests, keeping you financially in bondage–and them financially secured.

There are many who would make this statement concerning Abraham to support their doctrine on tithing. "Though it's not written in the Scriptures, Abraham tithed on a regular basis because God says this about Abraham": "I know him, that he will guide his children and his household after him, and they shall keep the instructions of the LORD–to deal honestly in all manner of judgment; that the LORD may bring to pass every word that had been spoken concerning Abraham (Genesis 18:19); because Abraham obeyed God's voice, and kept his charge, commandments, statutes, and laws" (Genesis 26:5). We know that it was the Sabbath that was given at creation (Genesis 2:1–3). But people will state, "Because Abraham kept God's Sabbath, we know he kept God's law of tithing as well."

Tithing Before the Law

As I have said before, people will take things out of context in the attempt to deceive you in believing this old covenant. Please observe this with me. The statement people will attempt to make: "Abraham kept God's Sabbath; He also kept God's law of tithing." Now, how could Abraham have kept God's law of tithing when *no laws (other than observing the Sabbath) even existed at this moment in time? No laws were given that established tithing* in the days of Abraham. The laws were not given until Moses' day.

So how did Abraham keep God's law of tithing when it was not yet given to man? I told you before how people use a lot of clichés with no Scripture backing, or if they use the Scriptures, they use them out of context (not referencing the purpose of mind relating to the text being described in the story). People will make these statements by using Scriptures out of context, and then form his/her own opinion as truth...and the sad thing about this is, many will follow likewise. So, according to the definition of the word "law," if tithing was before the law, which it was, then by definition we can say that there was no command, no rule, no precept, no custom, no legal directives or requirements to govern tithing. In

Hebrews 7:17, Jesus is referred to as having the same priesthood as Melchisedec (Greek spelling) and not after the manner of the Levitical priesthood. What does that mean? In the book of Hebrews 5:4-10, the bible affirms how God designated Christ to be a high priest similar to Melchizedek's priesthood. So, let's examine the similarities of both priesthoods:

Melchizedek's priesthood:

- referred to as a priest and king

- described as having a perpetual priesthood

- he was not a priest from the descendants of Levi; therefore, it was not mandatory for him to collect tithes

- there were no laws that governed or required tithing in those days

Christ's priesthood:

- referred to as a priest and king

- described as having an everlasting priesthood

- he was not a priest from the descendants of Levi and you will not find in biblical history where Jesus ever collected tithes

- after the death, burial, and resurrection of Christ; because the laws were abolished through his death; there were no new laws established that governed or required tithing

Now, there's a true comparison – short and simple!

Now let's focus on the life of Jacob, the other example of a tithe being promised prior to the law. In Genesis 28:20-22, Jacob made an interesting vow to God stating that if God be with him, protect him, feed him, clothe him, and allow him to return to his father's place of dwelling in peace, he would then declare that the God of heaven and earth is the real God...is his God. Then Jacob took a stone and set it up as a monument (a declaration of promise) to God and affirmed that all that God gives him he would give a tenth in return. This is the very first account in the Bible that gives an enlightenment of someone promising to give a tenth, or tithe, of his personal possessions back to God. So how is this description different from the teachings in most Christian organizations? Let's examine.

First, Jacob begins to make a promise to God, stating that "If God will do this," and, "If God will do that," he would declare that the Lord will be his God. Then Jacob finishes his proposal to God by stating, "If you fulfill my earnest request and provide for me, then I'll give a tenth back to you." God honored Jacob's proposal and, additionally, God continued to honor this same principle of tithing throughout Israel's history. However, let's ask ourselves some reasonable questions. How did Jacob, in reality, give a tithe to God? Did he personally hand it to God? Did he tithe to a representative of God, such as an angel or priest? Did he take it to a temple? What we do know is this; there are no Scripture references that we can view that demonstrates how Jacob could have given a tithe to God, since at the time of Jacob's existence, there were no temples or Levitical priests. But there are examples throughout Israel's history that demonstrate how they've given a tithe to God.

In Deuteronomy 12:6-7, God instructed Israel to bring all of their offerings (of many types) and tithes, then God stated that they will eat what God has provided them (which included their own tithe) in the presence of the Lord. Then the Lord went on to state that you (the tither) will rejoice in all that you have labored for, you and your entire household, because God had blessed them. Did God bless Jacob? Yes! Do you think that God would require something different from Jacob than what he required from Jacob's own children? No! The phrase "children of Israel" is interpreted as the "children of Jacob" because God had changed Jacob's name from "Jacob" to "Israel" in Genesis 35:10, and as Jacob's wives began to have children, his children were being referred to as the "children of Israel" rather than the "children of Jacob," because God stated the he would no longer be known as Jacob.

Furthermore, in Deuteronomy 14:28-29, his people (the children of Israel) were instructed to bring the entire increase of their tithes (seed from the land, not money) and lay them inside the gates of their own place of dwelling. Then they were instructed by God to sit and eat and be satisfied with their own labor that God had provided them. Now doesn't that sound like the proposition that Jacob made with God? In addition, it was also required, as his people ate their own tithes, that they would invite the Levites (because they had no portion or inheritance with the other tribes of Israel), the foreigners (strangers that were living in their midst, their neighbors), to include the fatherless, and the widow to join them to eat and partake of their tithes. During the life and story of Jacob, we know that there were no Levites; however, we do know that there were strangers (or foreigners) who lived in his own household. We can also conclude that there were widows and those who were fatherless during the existence of Jacob.

Genesis 35:2

"So Jacob told everyone in his household, "Get rid of all your pagan idols, purify yourselves, and put on clean clothing."

Who were the "everyone in his household"? When Jacob had returned to his own native land after living over 20 years with his wives' father (Laban), the Scriptures inform us that Jacob had gained menservants and maidservants, such as "Bilhah and Zilpah," who were his wives' handmaids, and who also served as secondary wives to Jacob. These maidservants were not of Hebrew descent and anyone who was not born of Jacob's loins, or who were not born after the manner of the Hebrew race, were known as strangers or foreigners. So, according to biblical history, how could have Jacob tithed to God, or how could have God acknowledged a tithe from Jacob?

By partaking of a portion himself, and his family, in communion and thanksgiving to God, and by sharing his fortune with those who were unfortunate, poor, strangers, etc., as God had instructed his children (the children of Israel) to do according to biblical history and the earlier uses of the tithe found in Deuteronomy 12:7 and 14:29.

Now according to one of the true practices of tithing in reference to biblical history, do you think that you can tell your pastor or leader that you are planning to use your own tithes to enjoy, for the sake of your own family and those less fortunate, in which God has blessed you by the sweat of your own labor and still be a member of that church or organization? You may be able to get away with that practice once, or maybe twice, but to include that type of behavior on a continual basis; you're asking to be removed from that organization. But, again, if we are going to keep the tithing doctrine of old or stay true to the practice, how come we can't practice it in the same manner in which God originally set it up? If you are brave enough, try doing that in this day and time. When you attend church this Sunday, or whenever you attend, try asking your pastor or leader if you can eat your own tithe instead of giving it to the church. The one thing that we could not do was eat or use anything, any tithes, first fruits, or offerings that we vowed to give to God.

Please Note: The giving of tithes was totally different from the giving of first fruit offerings. These were two different types of offerings, and the phrase "the first fruits of all your increase" is not to be considered the same as the rendering of tithes, as people generally teach. In Deuteronomy 12:17, God's people were informed that they were not permitted to eat anything that was committed to God as a vow. However, in Deuteronomy 14:22-23, we could eat our own tithes, but we could not partake of those things that were vowed. The story of Ananias and Sapphira found in Acts 5 is a similar example of someone making a commitment and not following through on it. In conclusion, I truly believe that tithing was before the law, and I hope you agree with this one fact concerning tithing before the law: There were no commands or requirements that governed tithing in the days of Abraham and Jacob.

CHAPTER TWO

Mosaic Law:

The History of Tithing

efore we observe the Mosaic Law on tithing, we must first establish one true fact. There was a money system present in those days. Many people preach, teach, or say there was only a bartering system (of animals and materials) in those days and that people did not use money. That's a myth! From the book of Genesis to Revelations, there was always a money system established; however, it was not the only system or even the first established system, but indeed it was a system used for trading and purchasing. Gold and silver were commodities used as money. Abraham used money to purchase servants (Genesis 17:13). He also used money (400 shekels of silver) to purchase land (Genesis 23:12-16). Genesis 42:35 describes Jacob as using "bundles of money," to go buy food in Egypt. According to the book of Judges 16:5, Delilah was paid 1,100 pieces of silver from each person who was involved in getting Sampson to reveal the strength of his power as a Nazirite. We know that there are countless details and records on how kings, such as David and Solomon, used gold and silver as money. As stated earlier, money wasn't the sole bartering tool, but it was a very commonly used tool in those days.

Why is this point being made? Because, when it came down to the tithe, "money" was never established as the commodity to use for it (though it was available to use). THE TITHE WAS NEVER MONEY. In the book of Exodus, Chapter 35, when Moses and the Israelites prepared to build the tabernacle, the offering accepted to be used to construct the tabernacle consisted of gold, silver, bronze, and other materials; however, "the tithe" (from the book of Genesis to Revelations) never consisted of money (though there was a money system present in those days). When Abraham gave a tenth of all the spoils to Melchizedek, the priest of the most high God, he gave of FOOD and POSSESSIONS.

Furthermore, when the tithe or tithing was instituted in the law, **FOOD** was the only commodity (of land, cattle, and the fruit of the tree) mentioned. When the law of tithing was instituted in the Law of Moses (Leviticus 27:30-33), it stated that all the tithes of the land, whether the seed yielded from the land itself or whether it yielded from the fruit of the trees, belonged to the Lord and should be considered "hallowed" or "holy" to him. Though there was a money system in place, tithes of money or possessions were never asked for by God. The above passage doesn't state a tithe of money was the Lord's, or that money could be accepted as a tithe. This is a very important passage of Scripture; "the Genesis of tithing," for it will be a very important text used when discussing the Malachi prophesies of tithes and offerings.

The tenth of all produce, flocks, and cattle was declared to be sacred to the Lord. However, for those who were willing, they were at liberty to take back and use the tenth of the grain or fruit that they gave as a tithe, but were required to pay back the full value of the amount borrowed with an added 20% (which was also known as the fifth part, which is 1/5 of 100% (Leviticus: 27:30-33). In other words, the mosaic law of tithing PERMITTED people to use their tithes for personal reasons; however, they were required to give a little extra on top of their tithes in return. If the practices of tithing today are equivalent to the practices of old, why then are people not allowed to use their own tithes, if and when needed? Why are many being told that if they don't tithe when they get paid/gain financial increases, they will be "cursed with a curse," if they use their tithe money for personal uses. According to the Mosaic Law, the people were at liberty to use their own tithes.

Furthermore, if a herdsman had only nine cattle, he/she was not required to tithe. When it came down to the tithe, God only required the tenth (1/10). It was not the first of the tenth, but rather the tenth of the tenth that belonged to the Lord, unlike many teachings that hint that the first tenth always belongs to God. As stated earlier, the giving of tithes is not the same as the giving of first fruit offerings and the first fruits of all your increase is not to be considered the same as the rendering of tithes (because the attributes of the tithe is the "tenth" and not the "first"). Remember, God did not even require the best of the cattle; we are talking about tithing and not sacrificing animals (for the sacrifices always had to be without blemish). The tithes were required from the LAND, not the air or the sea. So those who hunted wild birds and those who fished as a profession were not required to tithe. It was the "seed" or agricultural products from the fields that was sacred to God and tithable. Products from "trees" were to be tithed. This not only included the fruit, but oils, etc., of "herds or flocks." It was the "tenth" that passed under the rod that was holy and dedicated to God.

The law did not specify the various fruits of the field and of the trees that were to be tithed; however; they included everything edible, everything that was stored, or that grew out of the earth. The Pharisees, as early as the time of Jesus, made the law to consist of household herbs, such as mint and cumin (Matthew: 23:23; Luke 11:42), which was not something implemented by God but established later on as they (the leaders of that day) deemed fit. With regard to animal tithes, the law prescribed that every tenth animal that passed under the staff, which the shepherd orchestrated as he counted his flock, was to be sacred to the Lord, both good and bad alike. A tenth was ordered to be handed over to the Levites as a reward for their services to God and it was further ordered that the priests themselves dedicate a tenth of these goods they received to the devotion and maintenance of the high priest. In Numbers 18:21-28, a tenth of a tenth from the 10% of what the Levites gathered in, 1% went to the high priest. Now according to the practices of old, if we are really keeping these tithing regulations, your bishops, pastors, modern-day apostles (our high priests in today's society, as we so call them) should only be receiving 1% of the increase that comes into the church funds (if we are going to keep the old testament tithing requirements 100% WHOLESOME. This means if your church grosses $100,000 annually, your leader should only have received $1,000 (1%) from the church's funds that entire year (not 60% to 85%). So, if we are going to keep the tithing doctrine as a command for today, make sure that your leaders are doing their part to participate according to the entire law of tithing.

The legislation of tithing had been extended in the book of Deuteronomy for a period of time, and commands were given to the people to bring their tithes, together with their devotions and other offerings and first fruits, to the chosen place of worship. These tithes were to be eaten during celebration in companionship with their children, their servants, the fatherless, widows, foreigners, and the Levites (Deuteronomy 12:5-18). All the produce of the soil was to be tithed every year, and these tithes, along with the firstlings of the flock and herd, were to be eaten in the urban area. But, in case of distance, authorization was given to the nation of Israel to convert the produce into money, which was to be taken to the appointed place of worship and there the money was converted back to food for a festal celebration, in which the Levite was to be included [Deuteronomy 14:22-27]. The money itself was not given to the priest; the priests were never given money as a tithe. If we're going to follow the old covenant of tithing, we must do it right. We cannot use the excuse that there was not a money system established in those days, because there was, however the law stated:

Deuteronomy 14:22-26

"You must set aside a tithe of your crops–one-tenth of all the crops you harvest each year. Bring this tithe to the designated place of worship– the place the LORD your God chooses for his name to be honored–and eat it there in his presence.

"This applies to your tithes of grain, new wine, olive oil, and the firstborn males of your flocks and herds. Doing this will teach you always to fear the LORD your God. Now when the LORD your God blesses you with a good harvest, the place of worship he chooses for his name to be honored might be too far for you to bring the tithe.

"If so, you may sell the tithe portion of your crops and herds, put the money in a pouch, and go to the place the LORD your God has chosen. When you arrive, you may use the money to buy any kind of food you want–cattle, sheep, goats, or wine. Then feast there in the presence of the LORD your God and celebrate with your household."

The children of Israel were given an opportunity to exchange their cattle for money; however, the passage does not state that they took the money in their hands and gave it to the priest. Here is an opportunity for the law and Scriptures to demonstrate to us that money was given as a tithe (in their modern-day economy when money was also established). With this opportunity to use money as a tithe, the passage of Scripture continues to point out that the children of Israel were given permission to use the money received in exchange to purchase cattle, to offer a tenth to the priest, and to enjoy their tithes with their families–and, yes, they **ate their own tithes**. If God did not establish money as a tithable commodity (and money was present in those days), why are we establishing money as the only tithable commodity in today's society?

I know people will say that we can't use cows to pay the church's rent? And I will agree. However, that doesn't change the fact that the tithes were never established as money. Furthermore, I will address the purpose of the freewill offerings and its uses for the need of the modern-day church.

In Deuteronomy 14:28-29, at the end of three years, all the tithes from that year were gathered and laid up within the "gates" to be celebrated with the entire nation of Israel, to include the stranger, the fatherless, the widow, and the Levites. It was legislated that after collecting the tithes every third year, "the year of tithing," every Israelite had to proclaim that they had done their very best in fulfilling God's divine law (Deuteronomy 26:12-14). It is clearly seen in the Old Testament writings that as the use of the priesthood slowly weakened, so did the use of the customary tithing system and the observation of the law. However, these practices had extended into the later period of Jewish history and were partially maintained among the religious leaders as recorded in Matthew 23:23 and Luke 18:12. And, yes, Christ did state that these Pharisees (the keepers of the law) did give a tithe of:

- **mint** (garden herbs–used for sweet smelling)

- **dill/anise** (used as spices)

- **cumin** (seeds that have a warm, bitter taste and an aromatic flavor)

These practices were things that the Pharisees were supposed to do (as keepers of the law) without excluding other duties of the law, for there are no accounts where

Jesus or his disciples ever paid tithes. For Jesus' exact words ending his statement to the Pharisees, according to what was written, were:

Matthew 23:23

"But you ought to have done these, and not to have left the other undone."

Jesus did not state "for we ought to have done these things" but "for you ought to have done these things." Again, there are no accounts where Jesus or his disciples ever paid tithes. And, if you believe that Jesus was confirming that we should pay tithes then we should not be using money as the tithe, but using mint, dill, and cumin. Furthermore, in this New Testament account, the Pharisees did not give money as a tithe. Though the Pharisees offered/gave Judas money to betray Jesus (30 pieces of silver), it is not recorded that these Pharisees ever gave one piece of silver as a tithe (Matthew 26:14). How is it that these Pharisees gave money to betray Jesus but didn't give money as their tithes? In addition, the practices of tithing from the Pharisees had continued until the new covenant had come into effect (which took place at the death on the cross).

This will be discussed in more details in the latter part of this book.

CHAPTER THREE

THE MALACHI

PROPHESY

Those book of Malachi is the last book of the Old Testament; it has four chapters and 55 verses, according to what has been recorded and written. However, on most Sundays you will only hear the following verses:

Malachi 3:8-10

"Should people cheat God? Yet you have cheated me! But you ask, 'What do you mean? When did we ever cheat you?'

"You have cheated me of the tithes and offerings due to me. "You are under a curse, for your whole nation has been cheating me.

"Bring all the tithes into the storehouse so there will be enough food in my Temple. If you do," says the LORD of Heaven's Armies, "I will open the windows of heaven for you. I will pour out a blessing so great you won't have enough room to take it in! Try it! Put me to the test!"

As we observed in this passage, God stated that he was being cheated (in other biblical references the word "robbed" is used). Of what? Tithes and offerings! But who was God addressing when he stated "for you are cheating or robbing me"? Then God went on to say "your whole nation." There were two audiences God was addressing when he stated that he was being swindled of tithes and offerings. Keep in mind, we are addressing tithes of the land, whether of the seed of the land or of the fruit of the trees, as we have clearly defined, and not money. We know that when God spoke of the whole nation it is evident that he was addressing the nation of Israel and their practices. But what many don't know is that the immediate audience that God was addressing were the priests; they were required to receive the tithes for the services of God's house. Now if these priests were only required to receive the tithes (according to the law), why did God say that the priests were also guilty of robbing him? Maybe it's because the priests did not used what they received from the people for God's purposes only. Maybe the priests took a little here and took a little there for their own personal uses. This is just an opinion, but we will revisit this idea later.

What is the real message of Malachi's prophecy for believers today? Will you or anyone be "cursed with a curse" for not tithing? Let's define the phrase "cursed with a curse." These two words look identical, but they actually have different meanings. This will also clear up the thought that the general population of people (as preached) was cursed twice for not tithing. The first word "cursed" means to lay under a curse; to be made a curse; and to put on a curse, according to the Hebrew definition. The second word "curse" means to execrate, which means to be declared evil or detestable and to denounce. When we put it all together, this is what Malachi 3:9 means: For you lie under a curse and are declared evil or detestable for robbing me, the priests, and the whole nation of Israel. In proper translation, we see that they (the priests and Israel) were not cursed twice for not tithing (along with the offerings), but that they lay under a curse and were declared evil. What made the priests and the whole nation of Israel cursed? When you begin to read Malachi 1:14 and in Malachi 2:2 (prior to reading Malachi 3:9), they were already consider cursed. How? Why? Read Deuteronomy Chapter 27 and Chapter 28; God specifically stated to his people what causes the curses to come into their lives and what causes the blessings to overtake their lives.

God addressed the priests in Malachi 2:7-9, telling them that they are supposed to keep knowledge (God's ordinances and ways upright), but they were partial in keeping the law. This is why I injected the thought that maybe the priests took a little here and took a little there for their own personal uses because God pointed out that the priests were also guilty of robbing him (when they received the tithes from the people) in that they were partial in keeping the law (in not using the tithes and offerings for what they were intended). And remember, this was just a thought! In Malachi 2:17, God addresses them again on the fact that they have perverted the judgment of God by saying to those who did evil that they were doing well in the sight of the Lord. Deuteronomy 27:19 states that continual curses shall be upon everyone who alters the proper judgment rendered of God, whether they are strangers, fatherless, and widows. So what cursed the priests and the whole nation of Israel? Was it their tithes and offerings alone? Or was it them not keeping what God commanded in the book of Deuteronomy as described in the Law of Moses?

Another interesting point is that the blessings and the curses upon God's people were strictly based upon their commitment and obedience to God and his commandments. Prior to the book of Malachi, the book of Deuteronomy 28:1-2 and verse 15 points out that God's people were required to keep the entire law-that is if they wanted to receive the blessings of the Lord, but warned that failure to carefully follow these laws would lead to a life of cursings, which is described as a life of being declared evil. In the book of Malachi, if you read the whole book, and not just Chapter 3:8-10, you'll see that the priests and the whole nation of Israel were cursed based on Deuteronomy 27:15 through 28:1-19, where the blessings and curses were proclaimed and pronounced to his people based on their commitment and obedience to him. (Blessed if you do this, cursed if you do that, and not based on tithing alone!)

Again, Joshua 8:34 reads:

"Joshua then read to them all the blessings and curses Moses had written in the Book of Instruction."

It is amazing that most Christians think that the only thing of value in the book of Malachi are these three verses on "robbing God" and "receiving a blessing."

Malachi 3:10

"Bring all the tithes into the storehouse so there will be enough food in my Temple. If you do," says the LORD of Heaven's Armies, "I will open the windows of heaven for you. I will pour out a blessing so great you won't have enough room to take it in! Try it! Put me to the test!"

Many people tithe just for the sake of expecting mystical blessings from heaven in the form of cars, lands, houses, money, and becoming rich like their leaders. Therefore, we will observe the message behind the "windows of heaven." However, let's start off with Scriptures found in the book of Malachi, which are often overlooked; it's the set of Scriptures that follows the verses always mentioned:

The Malachi Prophesy

Malachi 3:11-12

"Your crops will be abundant, for I will guard them from insects and disease. Your grapes will not fall from the vine before they are ripe," says the LORD of Heaven's Armies.

"Then all nations will call you blessed, for your land will be such a delight," says the LORD of Heaven's Armies."

Now, let me repeat verse 12 to you once more; however, this time I will use the Hebrew definitions in place of certain words: "All nations shall pronounce you joyful because of who you are as a people, and your land will be such a place of enjoyment that everyone everywhere would want to come and be a part of, says the LORD of Hosts." God is not interested in people looking at your material things and identifying God in the many things that you have or own; Jesus even stated in Luke 12:15 to protect yourself from every kind of self-indulgence and that life is not calculated by how much you own or how much you have, neither does life consist of nor derive from possessing overflowing wealth over and above a person's necessities. As acknowledged in Malachi 3:12, God wants his people to be identified by

The Malachi Prophesy

the characteristics that define who God is (God's love, joy, peace, etc.), which ultimately spills over into everything you do, even where you dwell. We know God can get angry, but his characteristic is not anger but love, joy, etc. So in Malachi 3:12, God wants to be seen and known in and through his people (HIS characteristic traits demonstrated in the lives of his people).

God also promised them in verse 11 that their crops will be abundant and the he will guard them from insects and diseases; and that their grapes will not fall from the vine before they are ripe. Insects and diseases were the things that devoured (ate up and destroyed) the fruit of the ground and the fruit of the trees. But what causes the fruit to drop from the vine before it is ripe?

Let's focus on two main features of Malachi 3:10:

- **"The windows of heaven"**
- **"Pour you out a blessing"**

There are only two Scriptures in the entire (King James Version) of the Bible besides Malachi 3:10 that reference "the windows of heaven." Genesis 7:11 and Genesis 8:2 describe that during the life of Noah the windows of heaven opened up and flooded the earth with rain, and when the windows of heaven were stopped, the rain was restrained. In both of these instances, what came out of the "windows of heaven"? The answer is rain. Water is the key element that is required to protect the fruit from dropping from the vine before it is ripe. In this set of verses, why was God more interested in reviving their land? Because the fruit of the land was where the tithes were produced and manufactured. God was protecting his assets, the assets of the fields from which He required the tithes (the ground, the cattle, etc). As stated earlier, God said that he will guard their land them from insects and diseases. But what can God provide that will not cause their fruit to fall from the vine before it is ripe? We know that crops dry up and fall when there is a lack of water. When God stated that he will open the windows of heaven to pour out a blessing, God was referencing rain, not a Mercedes Benz, Lexus, or BMW, but simply rain. For it was rain that God had promised in many passages of Scriptures that he would provide for his people (for their lands) if they were to be obedient. Leviticus 26:4 states that God will send rain

The Malachi Prophesy

so the land can yield its crops and the trees of the field can produce their fruit. In Deuteronomy 11:14, 17, God promised seasonal rain that the people would be able to gather in the grain, the new wine (which is associated with the fruit of the grape), and the oil. Furthermore, God stated that if his people turn away from him and do not serve him then his anger will be against them, and he will shut up the heavens so that there will be no rain and the land will not yield its fruit. In Deuteronomy 28:12, God considered the giving of rain to his people as "His good treasury." Also, observe I Kings 8:35.

Rain cannot be spiritualized, though many will say that rain represents a type of the Holy Spirit; however, there are no Scripture texts that support that information. Anointing oil was used in the Scriptures and can be referenced as a type of the Holy Spirit. But rain cannot. Rain is simply rain. So, if you are a dedicated tither, and you are waiting for the windows of heaven to open up so God can pour you out a blessing, my question is, how can rain help you pay your mortgage, car note, or anything else? The purpose of rain as we have seen was for the seed to yield its fruits. How long will you be waiting for those things to come out of heaven?

Obviously, many leaders around you are not waiting for things from heaven when they can get those things from you. To sum up this information on tithes and offerings in the book of Malachi: We are not required to live according to the Levitical priesthood under the Law of Moses. We must always keep in mind that when the Bible says "tithes" it means products from the land, such as grains and cattle and not money. Because greed is so prevalent in this dispensation of time, many required the tithe to be paid in the form of money, so it became necessary to change the biblical use of the word "tithes" to now include money. If "money" can now be publicized to be a tithable commodity, then every believer (even nonbelievers) of every profession in the whole world will be compelled and required to pay ten percent of his/her income to the church establishment, ministry, or organization in order to be blessed, favored, and protected by God.

This increases the financial efficiency for ministry use (which is good, when done correctly) and for personal use, extremely high; and, the majority of these tangible increases will be seen and used for personal gain first, and everything else is secondary. Just start observing and don't be troubled by surveying your surroundings. But, according to Malachi 3:10, WHY did God want these tithes of the land brought to the "storehouse" (the granary)? Based on the information described in this text: "That there may be meat [bread] in Mine house." God wanted these tithes and offerings (grain) stored in the granary for the purpose of bread in His house. There is no spiritual application to these statements; these are to be taken as plainly viewed. Why should the people bring the tithes to the "storehouse" (a granary for storing grain) if the priests, who received the tithe, did not use it for its intended purpose, which was so that God can have "bread in His house"?

Remember, the writer of the book of Malachi didn't state that the priests didn't make enough bread for God's house. The author stated that they were guilty of robbing God of tithes (grains to produce the bread) and offerings. Now do you really imagine that God is chastising and cursing his people through Malachi's prophecy because we are not bringing enough money to church so that there may be more money in the house of God? Nevertheless, this is the message that is being broadcasted every Sunday morning.

Today's explanation of Malachi 3:10: "Bring all the tithes (money only) and extra offerings of money to the church," is inaccurate, yet there will be many by the thousands who will be willing to inspire you with their stories on how blessed they are (in every attainable physical, earthly, and material thing) once they became tithers. Furthermore, if many are willing and not afraid to testify of reality, there could easily be many by the hundreds of thousands who could tell you that tithing has not changed their financial status, not one bit. I'm blessed because of who God is and not because of what I can give to an organization. God does not view us as Levites (priests) described according to the Law of Moses but, more so, God views us as Christ's royal priesthood according to the new covenant. These two priesthoods are not the same (the Levitical priesthood and Christ's priesthood).

Here are a few of the main facts regarding the biblical history of tithing:

- Land owners were required to tithe

- Products of the land were the tithable commodity

- Only Levites could receive the tithes

- Tithing was later instituted in the Law of Moses

- Christians are not under the Law of Moses

- Money (silver and gold) was not used as a commodity of tithing.

CHAPTER FOUR

THE NEW TESTAMENT AND TITHING

I n the New Testament, the words tithe and tithing appears approximately eight times. In the book of Matthew 23:23, Luke 11:42, Luke 18:12, and Hebrews 7:5-6, 8-9; all of these passages refer to Old Testament usage and current Jewish practices. Nowhere in the New Testament are there any suggestions or commands for Christians to tithe. However, as believers we are to be generous in sharing our material possessions with the poor, and for the support of Christian ministry and various charities (meaning those who profess Christianity should find a way to assist and serve others freely, not looking for personal fame nor fortune). Christ Himself is our model in giving. Giving is to be voluntary, willing, and cheerful in the light of our servitude to God. Giving should not be systematic, and by no means limited to the giving of money only. We recognize that all we have is from God. We are called to be faithful stewards of all we have from God (including ourselves). Giving is sacred and should be continued in every good form. "For God so loved the world that He gave..." John 3:16.

As you see, what God has given us is much more than money; let us never perceive money as the only way to give. You can give of your time, talent, and, more importantly, of yourself. Yes, money should also be used as a tool to give, as it was in the book of Exodus; and, the people were willing to give gold, silver, and materials, and those who were skilled, in performing the workmanship for the use of constructing the tabernacle of God. And how to give is just as important as what to give! II Corinthians 9:7-8 informs us that we must personally decide in our own heart how much to give, not giving with a grudge, or giving because of the pressure or persuasion by the cunningness or craftiness of others. For God takes pleasure in those who give freely and cheerfully. You should never be forced to give or be manipulated to give at any time. You should never be made to feel embarrassed about the amount you give, as long as you are giving with a cheerful heart. I know that bills need to be paid in ministries, as well as the need of continual support for those who are less fortunate. So as you have the opportunity to give your money, time, and talent, do so in a willing and generous way.

As we continue to understand the emphasis of tithing in the New Testament, let's start by using these famous words spoken by Jesus, found in the book of **Matthew 5:17-18.**

"Don't misunderstand why I have come. I did not come to abolish the Law of Moses or the writings of the prophets. No, I came to accomplish their purpose.

I tell you the truth, until heaven and earth disappear, not even the smallest detail of God's law will disappear until its purpose is achieved."

The New Testament and Tithing

Let's look at two interesting words in this Scripture. The word "abolish," which has the same meaning as the word "destroy," which means to render in vain, to deprive of success, or bring to naught. The word "fulfill," which is the expression most often used, means to achieve, bring to pass, or accomplish sayings, promises, and prophesies. This word also means to complete, bring to an end, and expire (according to the Greek definition). So when Jesus stated, "I come not to abolish or destroy the law or the prophets but to fulfill," according to the Greek definitions, Jesus was saying that he came not to deprive the law of its success or render the law or the prophets vain, as if they or it never existed (how could he, God made the laws and influenced the prophets), but he came to bring to pass all the things that were prophesied of him and then bring the law to an end or expire it, because everything was now being fulfilled in him (Jesus Christ).

The Apostle Paul, who was an expert in the Law of Moses, understood Christ's purpose and his existence. Paul identified in the book of Romans 10:4, that Christ is the conclusion of the law (the boundary at which the law ceases to exist, for the law steered us in the direction of Christ, who is the completion of its existence.

There are no records found in the days of Christ where he required his disciples or followers, both men and women, to pay tithes; nor are there any records showing Christ receiving any tithes from anyone. Furthermore, there are no legitimate manuscripts anywhere that show Jesus (as a born Jew) ever paid tithes to anyone. Finally, there is no information in the entire New Testament Scriptures showing that new believers (Gentiles and not Jews who practiced the law) were taught or required to tithe. But many did spend a lot time with the Messiah and gave of themselves. Out of all the laws given to Israel contained in the first five books of the Bible, other than the Ten Commandments, "tithing" is practically the only other law that the present church attempts to maintain. They hold on to it in theory only; however, there is absolutely no similarity between modern tithing and the common practices of tithing under the Law of Moses except for the characteristic of 10%.

Christian tithing is a new-age enhanced feature of biblical taxation, and apart from the 10% aspect, it has

The New Testament and Tithing

nothing in common with the tithing practices regulated under the law. Not only is Christian tithing taught to be required, it is taught as a divine, binding LAW required directly from God himself. But there is no such thing as a "Christian tithing law" in the New Testament Scriptures. Tithing is not essential, but it is mandated by many leaders as a requirement, in some cases as if it's a requirement for salvation and, in most places, it is a requirement in order to become a member of that organization or ministry. Many are threatened and forced through various ways to surrender 10% of their salaries in obedience to this custom. For those who do not pay this 10%, they will be labeled as cursed and will be segregated (in friendship and fellowship between family and friends) from all the other tithers for fear that they will be cursed just by being around nontithers. All those who do not tithe are looked upon as filth and worthless, and are unable to participate in church functions, such as serving as a representative of that organization, church, or ministry.

Again, as mentioned before, you will not find any Scripture examples where anyone in the churches of the apostles gave a tithe, other than the law keepers (the

Pharisees), who were still under the law. You will not even find the Pharisees tithing after the death, burial, and resurrection of Christ. We have scriptural proof that no such law or custom as Christian tithing was taught or practiced in the church by the early apostles. Their epistles are totally devoid of any such tithing custom or law. In Ephesians 2:20, it states that together we are the dwelling place for God that has been constructed by the foundation of the apostles and prophets, where Christ himself is the chief component. And, again, you will never find where the apostle and prophets of the New Testament ever laid a foundation for tithing.

The early church converts were never taught to tithe to anyone. In the Jerusalem conference, found in the book of Acts 15, we find outlined what the apostles all agreed was necessary for the newly converted Gentiles to practice by inspiration of the Holy Spirit. Tithing is noticeably omitted. There were some believing Pharisees who wanted the apostles to teach the Gentiles to keep the Law of Moses (which certainly contained the law of tithing, Acts 15:5), but the apostles guided by Peter, James, Paul, and the elders of Israel would not consider that option (Acts 15:28-29). Yet what is one of the very first lawmaking duties taught to new believers in today's churches? YOU MUST TITHE! I can only speak for myself, as I have stated earlier, that my salvation and commitment to God is based on the confession and repentance of my sins to Christ, with the added turning away from old practices to accept the ways and life of Christ. Whereas, there are many whose salvation is also based on those qualities to include their dedication and faithfulness to tithing.

In Acts 5:1-4, a man by the name of Ananias, whose wife's name was Sapphira, made a promise/vow to sell a piece land and donate the entire proceeds for the needs of the ministry. After selling the land, Ananias realized he made much more than he expected from the land that he sold. When he realized how much money he made by selling the piece of land, he conspired with this wife to keep some of that money, only bringing part of the money and not the entire amount as earlier promised to God. Then the passage states:

Acts 5:3-4

The New Testament and Tithing

"Then Peter said, "Ananias, why have you let Satan fill your heart? You lied to the Holy Spirit, and you kept some of the money for yourself. The property was yours to sell or not sell, as you wished.

And, after selling it, the money was also yours to give away. How could you do a thing like this? You weren't lying to us but to God!"

The irony of this story is Ananias and Sapphira promised to give some of their proceeds from selling their land for the purpose of the church (the people and not the building). When they sold their land, they received more for it than what they anticipated. The sin wasn't the fact that they were supposed to have given all the money, the sin was Ananias and his wife withdrew secretly and appropriated the price for which they sold the land. (They lied about the price for which they sold the land and kept back part of the money; remember from the earlier information about when you make a vow to the Lord, you must pay up.) Now let's take a look at some very interesting points. Ananias and Sapphira sold their land and received money for their property. Why didn't the apostle Peter instruct them to tithe 10% from the money received from the sale? In Acts 5:4, Peter told Ananias that his property (the sold land) still belonged to him under his own control. Peter went on to say that even after the land was sold, the money gained from the sale was still at his own disposal and under his own management. But, the fact that he lied about the amount made from the sale was the real issue. Now

I have heard people use this passage of Scripture out of context by stating that Ananias and his wife were cursed because they failed to pay their tithes. Now how could that be a tithe? How can a tithe be at your own disposal and under your control to give? Is that what we hear preached around the world on Sunday mornings in the pulpits of our churches about tithing? "Saints, it is at your own disposal and under your own control to pay tithes." But, rather, you will hear, "If you don't pay tithes then you are cursed with a curse." The Holy Spirit never exacted or reprimanded Ananias and Sapphira for not paying tithes.

If you ever read about the rich young ruler found in the book of Matthew 19:16-22, Jesus told this rich young ruler to sell his possessions and give to the poor. This man was not instructed from Jesus to give 10% tithe of the proceeds from his possessions (if sold) to the church, but rather, all was to be given to the poor. If we say that we're going to live not by bread alone, but by every word that proceeds out of the mouth of God, then let's practice it. Notice this Scripture quoted from Matthew 4:4 said that we should live by the proceeding word, which means, not only what God had said, but what God is also now saying. In Genesis 22:2, God told Abraham to sacrifice his only son on the mountain of Moriah. Then the angel of the Lord said to Abraham in Genesis 22:12, not to sacrifice Isaac or do any harm to his child. If Abraham had only obeyed the proceeding Word of God, he would have killed Isaac, his son. Let me ask you, how many Isaacs have you killed based on things you believe God had said, but not what God is saying now? Both are important. What God had said and what he is now saying.

In Luke 10:4, Jesus told his disciples, as he sent them on a mission, not to take bags or sandals and not to greet anyone on the road; then, in Luke 22:35-36, Jesus told his disciples to go get bags and if they don't have one then buy one. My question to you is, what was the last word you heard the Lord say? The Bible states in the book of Hebrews 1 that in times past he had communicated with his people through the prophets of old, but concluded that in these final days, He (God) has spoken to us through His son (Christ). So, if that's the case, what has Christ said and is saying to us through his written word? One thing I know for sure is, he never spoke anything about Christian tithing.

People have suggested that tithing is to be understood (no scriptural backing) among the Jews and therefore didn't have to be repeated or talked about. Okay, let's say that was the case. Why didn't they pass that information on to the Gentile church? They were not born Jews; therefore, tithing would not have already been understood by the Gentiles. In the book of Acts, one of the Jewish believers went down and told the Gentile church in Antioch that in order to be saved they must get circumcised (Acts 15:1-31). There were certain men who departed from the church in Jerusalem (which consisted of Jews lead by Peter, James, and John) who taught the believers in the Gentile church that if they were not circumcised, they were not saved (despite them accepting the message of Christ). When Paul and Barnabas heard about this, they strongly disagreed with that message. Then Paul and Barnabas went to the source of where that (Jewish practice) statement originated. Paul and Barnabas went straight to the church in Jerusalem to speak to the apostles and the elders about that message. Then the Scriptures go on to say this, "But there rose up certain of the sect of the Pharisees which believed saying that it was needful to circumcise them, and to command them to keep the Law of Moses" (Acts 15:5).

Acts 15:24

"We understand that some men from here have troubled you and upset you with their teaching, but we did not send them!"

Because of this statement, the apostles and elders came together to consider this law commanded to the Gentiles to follow. Now look at this. There were some believing Pharisees (who followed some of Christ's teachings) and were in communion with other Jewish believers in Jerusalem. (For Paul didn't' go to where the Pharisees congregated to debate with them, but he went to the church in Jerusalem because there were believers who came from among them who implemented this rule to the new Gentile converts). After much discussion and debate between Peter, James, John and the elders of Israel - they came to the conclusion that they would not put a yoke upon the neck of the disciples (Gentiles) and the only advice they were willing to give the Gentiles was that they should *"withdraw from polluting themselves with idols, abstain from fornication, and stay away from things strangled from blood (a Jewish practice)."* No mention of tithing!! How about that? Out of all the things/observances that needed to be passed on to the Gentile church, tithing was not one of them.

See, in Matthew 23:23, the Pharisees kept the law of tithing because they were law keepers. Jesus didn't confirm tithing in this text of Scriptures, he only acknowledged what the Pharisees (law keepers) were supposed to do and that was to uphold and maintain the keeping of the law. Jesus didn't start this text of Scripture by stating, "Blessed are you, Pharisees," but rather, "Woe unto you, Pharisees, Hypocrites..." The two times in the New Testament that Jesus mentions tithing is in condemnation of the Pharisees. At the time of Jesus' ministry there was a temple and there was a Levitical priesthood; therefore, tithing was still in effect for the Jews only. Hear now the only words ever recorded of Jesus mentioning tithes (in the book of Matthew and Luke):

Luke 11:42

"What sorrow awaits you, Pharisees! For you are careful to tithe even the tiniest income from your herb gardens, but you ignore justice and the love of God. You should tithe, yes, but do not neglect the more important things."

Now just what kind of a blessing did Jesus utter to these Pharisees for their tithing of mint and herbs? And what kind of blessing did Jesus utter to the Pharisee who stood and prayed, boasting about how much he fasts and gives tithes (Luke 18:12). None! No blessing pronounced from Jesus for tithing. What does being uttered a "hypocrite" and passing over "judgment" and the "love of God" have to do with "tithing"? That's the whole point. These gross sins have virtually nothing to do with tithing!

Tithing to Jesus was so absolutely insignificant to the gross sins of failing to properly judge the widows and orphans and fatherless and poor, and not demonstrating the love of God toward them. Tithing was the smallest and most insignificant thing Christ could think of to show the utter hypocrisy of these Pharisees. These Pharisees were thorough about tithing (a law of virtually no spiritual rewards), and yet ignored things like judgment, love, and mercy. Let me repeat this fact: Christ stated that these Pharisees (the keepers of the law) did give a tithe of:

- **mint** (garden herbs – used for sweet smelling)

- **dill/anise** (used as spices)

- **cumin** (seeds that have a warm, bitter taste and an aromatic flavor)

And, again, these practices were things that the Pharisees were supposed to do (as keepers of the law) without excluding other duties of the law. Furthermore, I again encourage everyone to continue to give, being generous in sharing our material possessions with the poor and those who have need in support of Christian ministry and charities–not limited to the giving of money only.

Give to reputable charities if you have extra. Give to your neighbor in need. Give to your family members and relatives in need; give to a neighbor in financial distress.

Even when tipping someone, let it be a reflection of the one that you are representing in your Christian walk. And most importantly, give as God gives you the discernment and the ability to give. Our God is a generous God–may you become generous also. Develop a "love for freewill giving." Every ministry, church, synagogue, temple, etc., should learn to trust God by faith to provide money from voluntary gifts given from the heart as was demonstrated to us by the early church in the New Testament.

The ministry can be continued by trusting God by faith and using the freewill offerings to maintain the never-ending needs of the ministry. Faith, Faith, Faith is the essential element in order for any ministry to survive. As every ministry should freely give, then too should every ministry freely receive, not requiring people to give. Every established church should have enough faith and wisdom in appropriating their finances to maintain the establishment. The requirements for individual gain should be last in comparison to the needs of the ministry itself. As Peter and Paul trusted God to financially support their ministries, they also trusted people to freely be committed to their own ability to give.

The apostle Paul accepted freewill offerings to support himself (not becoming filthy rich) and for the poor saints in Jerusalem found in the book of Romans 15:26. Paul the apostle had a job. According to Acts 18:3, Paul was a tentmaker by occupation and worked with both Aquila and Priscilla, who also shared that same profession. If you make a promise to give then be loyal to your commitment; however, do not be forced to give or forced to commit your loyalty to someone else's goals. The church should be financially sustained by freely giving and freely receiving and trusting God by faith to preserve them.

CHAPTER FIVE

THE OLD

VS.

THE NEW COVENANT

s we venture through this very interesting chapter, please keep in mind what was mentioned earlier when Jesus stated in Matthew 5:17-18, about how he came not to deprive the law of its success or render the law or the prophets vain as if they or it never existed, but he came to bring to pass all the things that were prophesied of him and then bring the law to an end, or expire it, because everything was now being fulfilled in him. There are three fascinating books of the Bible that coincide around the same period of time and that focuses on a particular subject. These three books are Acts, Galatians, and Hebrews, and one of the major subject topics of discussion in those days was the "significance of the law" in contrast to "grace and faith" established by Christ Jesus as the "new common practices" for believers. As we have read earlier in the book of Acts 15, how there were some believers who associated with Peter, James, and John and the established church in Jerusalem. These men traveled to Antioch of Pisidia, which encompassed the surrounding cities, such as: Lystra, Iconium, and Galatia and taught new believers in Christ that they must first follow the teachings of Judaism (the laws) prior to becoming Christians.

The book of Galatians is linked to this period of time because there were new believers (Gentiles) in Galatia who had believed the teachings of these men who had come from Jerusalem. Paul (the apostle) spent almost his entire message/writings to the Galatians, instructing them that they are not required to keep the law or practices to solidify their relationship with Christ. In Galatians 1, Paul informed the believers in Galatia how he was shocked that some of them (Gentiles) were turning away from Christ to follow a different teaching. What teaching? The teaching from those believers from Jerusalem who instructed the Gentiles that the real way to Christ comes from observing the laws. Paul went on to say their teachings are not the gospel that Christ left behind, the gospel that he (Paul) now preaches. He also stated to the new converts/believers in Galatia that they are being fooled by those who purposely twist the truth concerning Christ and announced: May God's curse fall on anyone who teaches a different message of hope and faith other than the message of Christ Jesus. Paul later affirms himself as a Jew and the understanding of the law and its functioning. In Galatians 2:19-21, Paul stated that when he tried to keep the law, it condemned him; therefore, he died to the law and no longer tried to meet all its requirements so that he might live for God. He went on to say that his old self (along with his old practices) have been crucified with Christ, and the life that he is now living is in the Son of God who loves him and died for his sins.

The Old vs. The New Covenant

Now that's where the book of Hebrews comes into play because this book speaks specifically about this new covenant based on the death, burial, and resurrection of Christ and what it means to us in relation to why Christ gave his life for us. There are many who would inform you that this book was written by the apostle Paul, Peter, James, Luke, or other authors; however, there is no historical information that could pinpoint the exact author. But what's more important is that this letter was written to the Jewish nation because of the repeated usage of Old Testament quotations concerning the law. The repeated warning against spiritual unbelief indentifies the concern for those Jews who were on the verge of renouncing Christianity and returning to their former practices–that is, living according to the Law of Moses. This book strongly emphasizes the identity of Christ as the Son of God, as one who is far superior to Moses and angels. It also emphasizes not to become restless in turning away from Christ and continuing in unbelief as many of their forefathers did under Moses. Finally, this book revisits the past practices of the law, only to conclude that Christ had established in office a new and better covenant by a new and living way, not according to past practices of the law.

The Old vs. The New Covenant

In recollecting their past practices, Hebrew 7 begins by describing Melchizedek and his encounter with Abraham as we have discussed earlier in the book. As you continue to read, the author points out that the tribe of Levi and all their descendants were tasked by God with the priestly office and were commanded, according to the law, to collect the tithes from all the other tribes of Israel. Then the author informs us that Melchizedek, who was a priest, however not according to the ancestry of the Levites (which means he was not bound or required by any law to collect tithes), accepted tithes from Abraham (the spoils that were collected during battle, including the items that belonged to the King of Sodom) and blessed him, not because of any tithes given because the tithes were not required, but he blessed Abraham because of the promises he had already received from God. As stated earlier, Romans 4:13 reminds us that the promises made to Abraham did not come through observing the commands of the law, but through the righteousness of faith. We all know that tithing is not an act of faith, it a stationary entitlement. Faith is the things we hope to attain without any evidence on how to obtain them (the things we are hoping for).

The giving of the tithe is attainable with no hope necessary based on the total amount of income you receive from one dollar to a million and beyond (according to today's practice of tithing). The author points out, to avoid all confusion, that Melchizedek, who was greater by deity, stature, and nature, blessed Abraham who was lower in nature, because he (Abraham) possessed something that no other person had at that time. What Abraham obtained wasn't based on tithes, but the author points out that Melchizedek blessed Abraham because he possessed the promises given to him directly from God–as indicated earlier–promises by the righteousness of faith. The writer then expresses the thought that many will say that the Levites (who were only required to collect tithes and not be required to pay them) paid them through Abraham, based on what Abraham gave Melchizedek. *(This is the concept from which many state that by tithing -- your children's children will be blessed)* Now this gets interesting.

For those who will attempt to make that claim concerning the Levites paying tithes made by Abraham, the writer points out that at the time when Abraham and Melchizedek met, Abraham was still attached to the loins of his forefathers. Who were Abraham's forefathers?

Joshua 24:2

"Joshua said to the people, "This is what the LORD, the God of Israel, says: Long ago your ancestors, including Terah, the father of Abraham and Nahor, lived beyond the Euphrates River, and they worshiped other gods."

So the writer wanted us to know that the claim cannot be made that the Levites paid tithes through the loins of Abraham, because Abraham, at the time that he met Melchizedek, was still connected to the loins his forefathers, who were a people who served other gods and who did not possess the promises from God. Our relationship to Abraham is based on faith, not so much as the way in which he lived or the acts nor accounts of his lifestyle. The writer goes on to state and pose an interesting thought: If flawlessness (a perfect relationship between God and man) had been attained by keeping the law through the Levitical priesthood, then why was it essential for another and different kind of priest (Christ Jesus) to come forth, one who was not attached to the family tree of the Levites, but to the tribe of Judah? When the law was written in the Old Testament, under Moses, there was no mention of any other priests being established for the services of God other than those from the tribe of Levi. Then the writer states in Hebrews 7:12 that anytime there is a change in the type of priesthood (which carries its own set of rules and practices), there is a necessity to amend the past practices of the law as well. If we are no longer under the rituals and requirements of the Levitical priesthood, but now under Christ's priesthood, why then are we still being required to tithe in accordance to the practices of the Levitical priesthood?

The passage of Scripture goes on and informs us that Christ's priesthood was not constituted on the basis of a bodily legal requirement, but on the basis of the power of an everlasting and imperishable life and that the previous physical regulations, commandments, and requirements are rescinded because of their weakness, ineffectiveness, and uselessness.

As we have established earlier, the tithes were also used to support the Levitical priesthood, because they were chosen to serve the Lord in his temple/tabernacle 24 hours a day, seven days a week, and the need to feed them was a necessity. But the passage of Scripture found in Hebrews 7:27 states that Christ has no day-to-day dependents, as did the other high priests, but has met all the requirements, once and for all, when he offered himself as a living sacrifice and died on the cross for all mankind. So here's the question: How and when did Christ fulfill the law by bringing it to an end? When was the old covenant (with its regulations) replaced by the new covenant (with its freedoms)? One thing I know for sure, Christ did not come to relive the law but bring it (the law) to an end and expire it. In Hebrews 8:7, it informs us that if that first covenant had been without flaw, there would have been no room for another one or an attempt to institute another one.

Hebrews 8:8-10

"The day is coming," says the LORD, "when I will make a new covenant with the people of Israel and Judah. This covenant will not be like the one I made with their ancestors when I took them by the hand and led them out of the land of Egypt.

They did not remain faithful to my covenant, so I turned my back on them, says the LORD.

The Old vs. The New Covenant

But this is the new covenant I will make with the people of Israel on that day, says the LORD: I will put my laws in their minds, and I will write them on their hearts. I will be their God, and they will be my people."

The new covenant/agreement is the Lord living in us (in our earthly tabernacle), and He becoming our God and we becoming His people, and our service to him 24 hours a day in our bodily form. Hebrews 8:13 goes on to say that when God spoke of a new covenant or agreement; he purposely made the old covenant obsolete/out of order, and what he had established as being outdated is ready to be discarded and released. So when did the new covenant take precedence over the old covenant? Hebrews 9 tells us that the first covenant had its own rules and regulations and customs for common practices and sacrifices. Then it goes on to say that wherever a will and testament is written, that will cannot be implemented except by death of the one who has written and sealed the will. Furthermore, it states that a will and testament is valid and is activated only at death, being that the will has no strength or legal authority as long as the one who created the will is still living.

The old first covenant, under Moses, was inaugurated, sanctioned, and put into power by shedding the blood of animals. The law itself was cleansed by means of blood, and without the sacrifices of animals–using their blood to represent a discharge from sin and its guiltiness–the children of Israel would not be redeemed for their iniquities committed. So when did the new covenant take effect over the old? When was the new "will" put into effect? When did Christ shed his blood? That's right, at the cross!

The New Testament was not implemented during the time when Jesus walked the earth. When Jesus walked the earth, he was fulfilling prophecy. However, the New Testament was implemented at the death on the cross, where his blood was spilled and when the new will (covenant or testament) took effect (after his death). For the new "will" was put into practice due to the death of the one who wrote it.

So all these teachings about Christ confirming the tithing practices are inaccurate. Because the old covenant (practices of the law) was still in effect prior to his death, the Pharisees and the practice of tithing were still in effect. While Jesus yet walked the earth, as long as he was alive, the old covenant was in effect, and as long as he had not shed his blood the old covenant still reigned. It was at the death on the cross that the new covenant came into effect. Before Christ's death, the old covenant was transiting into the new covenant. Jesus' teachings surpassed that of the law, by a new and living way, by his death, burial, and resurrection. After Jesus Christ died for our sins, the new "will" had come into effect, and the promise of him living in us (permanently) had begun. This is why the apostle Paul struggled with the teachings of the law, as a continual requirement with the gospel of Christ.

Paul understood the law, the power, and its uses, but he also understood through the revelation from Christ the power of faith, grace, and righteousness and their uses, overriding the previous requirements. So his letters to the Galatians were pretty strong about NOT following the law as the way to mature in Christ, for Paul even stated that if righteousness had come by obeying the law then Christ's death would have been in vain, for Christ's death was a replacement of law and its practices. As many struggled in that day to convert over

The Old vs. The New Covenant

from the practices of the old way and accept the new direction, many today struggle in that same manner by refusing to let go of old practices to embrace this new and living way.

CHAPTER SIX

CULMINATION

T raditions can be summarized as beliefs, customs, principles, or values passed down from one generation to the next with the element of performing and retaining historical practices from its original roots. Traditions have always been a way of life for many people of all races, creeds, and colors. The observance of tradition plays a very important function for those who are destined to follow and maintain. Everyone practices some form of tradition, whether great or small, from simply the way you comb your hair or brush your teeth or something on a larger scale, such as: family reunions or celebrations. I personally enjoy traditional values that I inspire my children to sustain and pass down to their children. I like tradition when it's maintained in its proper place; however, when it comes to Christianity, the only tradition that should have any type of significant value should be Christ's spoken words. I tell people all the time that Old Testament writings are not the "law," but there is a "law" contained in the Old Testament, along with psalms, prophecies, love stories, and ancestries to encompass the countless examples of human behavior with chronological history.

The apostle Paul informed us in Romans 15:4 that there were many historical writings about God and his people, enough to conclude that these writings were maintained for our learning and displayed as an example for Christian behavior. Paul admonished the church in Corinth (I Corinthians 10:11) that the writings of old (which illustrated the character of those who faltered in their beliefs) were established for our caution, to warn us of the consequences for not serving God and to enlighten us about the benefits of following Christ for the rest of our natural existence. Traditions are good, but harmful when reverenced above God's word, and dangerous when given greater weight than the message of Christ. Tradition is an effective way to ineffectively serve God. There are many church traditions that infringe on biblical knowledge and truth; in some cases, traditional customs are more valuable and essential than biblical concepts. It is vital in the twenty-first century that we as a people reevaluate and separate personal traditions from Christian living, or learn how to incorporate good tradition with Christian living without eliminating the essence of Christianity.

I remember hearing a story where someone stated that during every Thanksgiving holiday, he and his wife would purchase a very expensive and nice-sized piece of ham. After seasoning the ham and prior to placing it in the oven, his wife would cut off large portions of the ham (usually both sides of the ham). Year after year, his wife practiced that routine, belief, and tradition. Then one day, he asked his wife, "Honey, why do you cut off both sides of the ham before positioning it in the pan?" She looked at him and responded, "Baby, I don't really know why. This is how my mother always prepared the ham, so I copied it." There was a point in time when he and his wife were in the company of his wife's mother, and his wife asked her mother why she cut off the ends of the ham before placing it in the pan. His wife's mother responded, "Sweetie, I don't really know why other than that was something mommy used to do." Fortunately, his wife's grandmother was still alive and there arose an opportunity when his wife asked her grandmother why she cut off the ends of the ham prior to placing it in the pan. Her grandmother answered, "Baby, that's because when I was little girl, we didn't have pans big enough to hold a large piece of ham, so my mother used to cut off the ends of the ham to fit the pan."

What is the moral of this story? This tradition and practice was being kept without the knowledge of why it was being continued, and for years a lot of ham was being wasted.

If you don't understand why you do what you do, you could fall into the trap of wasting years of your life. What practices and traditions are you holding on to without the full understanding behind these religious customs? It is time out for aimlessly doing things just for the sake of doing things. Start investigating your practices and question these behaviors that have kept you constrained for so long.

There was a practice or belief that God had established in the Old Testament writings and was validated by Christ during his lifetime–to support the poor and care for the widow. I am reminded about the parable that Jesus presented in reference to the rich young ruler who observed the commandments of God ever since he was a little child. But, somewhere in the heart of this rich young ruler, there was still a question of attaining eternal life, even though he practiced the commandments ever since he was young. Then, in the parable, Jesus expressed to the ruler that he lacked one small detail–and that was to sell his possessions and distribute the proceeds to the poor.

In this parable, Jesus' response to the ruler wasn't a punishment, but rather the expression of God's heart. The ruler was on a quest to gain something eternal from God, to posses a better relationship with God other than just keeping several commandments. The essence of the heart of God, as described in earlier writings, included meeting the needs of the poor, especially when you have the ability and resources to accomplish it. Again, Jesus expressed in Luke 12:15 that a man's existence is not based on how prosperous you can live, or based on how much you gain or possess in this life, but it is measured by our response to care for, aid, and support those who are in need, whether the need is spiritual and physical, especially those who are poor. It should be the desire for any Christian or Christ follower to please the one you are following by demonstrating his passion. Jesus' parable was not stating that every rich person should take their life's savings and give it to those who are less fortunate, because that would then place them in a similar state of necessity. But the parable implied that if you really want to become a follower of Christ, you must be willing to separate yourself from greed and be willing to give up those things that you esteem highly and deem precious. To become a true servant of God, we must empty ourselves of things that would cause distraction in our relationship with Christ.

You cannot be controlled and governed by worldly lusts and expect to have a fruitful relationship with God, because God will, as he indicated in the parable of the young ruler, show you the nature of your heart and challenge your will. One point I would like to employ: When Jesus asked the ruler to sell what he had, he didn't suggest that the ruler pay tithes from the proceeds of the money, or give a little to the temple or priests, or to even sow some of it in the treasury, but to give it all to the poor. What a true illustration of the heart of God!

Today, it seems as if the traditions of men have turned away from that form of giving. I witnessed many utter that the church is not a social service nor is it the responsibility of the church to care for the poor because Jesus stated, **"The poor you have always with you."** That remark from Jesus was not a statement to condemn the poor or a rule of thumb for not supporting the poor; but, according to the practices of Christ and the apostles, that statement would rather inform us of our responsibility to always take care of the poor because they will always be in our company. They are always with us and we should always help them–and that is why Christ told the rich young ruler to give his support to a class of people where there will always be needs. It seems that many have moved away from the heart of God by not reaching out and continuously helping those who are less fortunate with their material wealth. Yes, we will reach out with the Bible, but not things. The good treasure, as the rich young ruler demonstrated, was kept back and not shared.

We offer many excuses why we cannot reach out to the poor (even to those who are faithful members of the establishment or organization who experience lack on a daily basis), and at the same time we give many reasons why we should give more money to the church in support of a church vision that does not support or mirror the heart of God. And, yes, we do have to use the wisdom of God when determining those who have a true need from those who are ready to take advantage of the kindhearted and openhanded. What also comes to mind is the story about the poor widow woman found in the books and verses of Mark 12:42-44 and Luke 21:2-4. Many use these passages of Scripture out of context, teaching that it's God's will for the poor to give out of their need and in doing so that God will provide and replenish them. But in these passages of Scriptures, Jesus wasn't celebrating her; in fact, he was amazed to see that she was giving all that she had into this treasury instead of receiving from the temple and from this treasury. Again, when you look at history, God taught his people to support the widows and give to the poor.

The apostle Paul and many of the disciples were mindful of rendering their support to the widows and the poor with the alms that were gathered by those who gave. They were also mindful of instructing those who participated in Christian fellowship to support and aid those widows who were family members. Paul also stated to the Corinthian church as he was expressing his thoughts on giving, "...they that have little will have no lack." Again, this expression holds similar content to what Jesus told the rich young ruler "to give all to the poor."

So here you have this poor widow woman casting her life's savings into the treasury, giving all she had. This act demonstrated by the poor widow woman created an even greater deficiency in her financial status, confirming her neglect. And Jesus, standing there at the treasury, recognized how neglected she had been based on what she was casting into the treasury. He admitted that she had given more than all of them. However, Jesus never turned to his disciples and declared the way she gave as a model for giving; neither did he admonish anyone to give out of their poverty.

In fact, in my opinion, I believe that Jesus was overflowing with amazement that the temple was celebrated and esteemed greater than the needs of this poor widow. I believe that Jesus was grieved with the people who operated the temple because the people who had plenty were taking from this widow who had nothing, instead of encouraging those with plenty to support those with less and few.

Jesus was not applauding her efforts, he was just stating the obvious and he never commanded his disciples to give in that same manner. Furthermore, Jesus never stated that this poor widow was blessed because of the way she gave, that verbiage is not recorded in biblical history. People will attempt to use the parable of the talents (out of context) to support their greed by saying that Jesus took the talents from the person who had few and gave them to the one who had plenty. And, again, that parable had nothing to do with making the rich richer and the poor poorer; that parable was about people who waste their talents due to being lazy, as well as other reasons; Jesus used this parable to show that he'd rather you give your talents to someone who is going to do something with it, than to let it go to waste. It's as simple as that.

I was in a conversation with one of my favorite aunts just a few weeks ago; she was bringing me up to date on things that were occurring in her life. During our dialogue, she brought to my attention that she had just joined a new church and was giving $500 dollars from her state assistance check (because her new pastor had solicited her participation in giving) to support a guest speaker who was visiting the ministry over the next several days. So I began asking my aunt whether or not she had paid her bills yet (for the month) and she answered me with a solemn "no." So I began to question her good intentions with the reality of her circumstances, and I informed her that it is not a wise choice to offer money that had already been obligated toward paying her bills in exchange to appease someone else's conscience, or being well liked.

Then she stated that particular thought was in her mind, but she disregarded that notion and incorporated another rationale to defend her initial frame of mind to give the $500 dollars instead of paying her bills. She informed me that her other objective behind her giving was to offer this money as a "seed offering" to the Lord in hope that her daughter would receive salvation. Then I responded, "Seed money for salvation. Jesus doesn't need your money in exchange for salvation, and if he did $500 dollars would not be a sufficient amount." She chuckled then asked me, "Can you sow a seed in hopes of someone accepting Christ?" My response was, "I have never seen that message, a seed of money for salvation ever instituted during biblical times, but I do remember a passage of Scripture in the Bible that states, 'In every situation and in everything, by prayer and frequent petitioning with gratitude and thanksgiving, continue to make your desires known to God.' "

Furthermore, I plainly declared to my aunt, let us both pray that God would open up your daughter's heart to hear the message of salvation and that your daughter would allow Christ to come in and make his home in her life. Then I began to teach and enlighten my aunt about these strange doctrines of giving; but, more importantly, I hope and pray that my aunt wasn't afraid to respectfully inform her pastor that she doesn't have the money to give at this particular time based on that money being already obligated to meet the needs of her bills.

The Bible says in Matthew 15:1-6 that the Pharisees articulated to Jesus that his disciples violate the rules handed down by the elders of the past by not washing their hands before they eat. Jesus responded by asking them why they defy the commandments of God by observing the customs of their elders in greater reverence than the Word of God. Then Jesus explained to the Pharisees that the commandments of God instructed them to always honor their father and mother and don't mistreat them. Jesus went on to say, when your father and mother comes to you in need, you (Pharisees) say to them, I'm sorry I will not be able to assist you; the money that I have set aside for general use has been dedicated to the temple and given to God.

Therefore, I can't support your request and I am exempt and no longer obligated to honor you. Jesus ended his statement by saying that the traditions of the Pharisees and the rules passed down by their elders; they have deprived the Word of God of its force and authority and made it useless and powerless. Jesus indicated that God commanded us to honor our parents by supporting them in every way, shape, and fashion without neglecting their necessities. Even when it comes down to financial support, Jesus is not accepting the explanation that you can't help your parents because you have to pay your tithes and offerings, or that your money has been dedicated to the building fund. Jesus didn't accept that justification then, and he is not accepting it now. Everything we do in life must be done at the right time, in the right place, and in the proper order. Jesus never designed the practices of giving to our father or mother to be overwritten by the pretext of your gifts offered to the ministry.

Years ago, I remember a dear friend of mine, after some serious studying on the topic of tithing, decided to end his commitment to the law of giving 10%; devoting himself on becoming a stronger free will giver. In his excitement, he shared that information about his new found freedom with everyone he knew; however, his good news had sorely entered into the ears on his pastor. When he went to church that Sunday morning, he was summons to the pastor's office being bombarded and escorted by all the elders who acted as if they were the pastor's bodyguards rather than men of God. As my friend entered the pastor's office, there was a good buddy of his (the one who communicated this information to the pastor) sitting in the pastor's office looking sorrowful and confused. My friend vividly told me, "man I remember when I entered the office; the first person I seen was an old buddy of mine. Then I remember feeling as if I was in the court of law because the elders and the pastor began interrogating and chastening me for what I believed. But I caught them all by surprise, because they thought I would back down because of intimidation; however, I challenged them to observe the scriptures with me; but they refused too, stating that they don't have time for this stuff". After being held captive for about 45 minutes, my friend was released to go and instructed to enjoy the Sunday morning service. Now come on! It is not humanly possible to forget everything that just happened and immediately go on as if it never occurred. So, my friend stated as the pastor was ushered to the pulpit with his elders, he snatched the microphone from the stand and began stating that God told him there are people sitting in the congregation that are not tithers and that those who do not tithe is going to hell because all non-tithers are cursed. Then, he went on to say, if you want to be a non tither; you will curse and condemn your own family for eternity. Needless to say, my friend and his family are no longer associated with that ministry or any other ministry that agrees with that type of philosophy.

Just recently, I had a conversation with a gentleman who, after some serious studying, decided to break free from the bondage of tithing; just remaining a very attentive free-will giver. During our dialog, I asked him, "Does your pastor know about your decision?" He replied "no – he's currently in Africa". Then I made him aware of some things that his pastor may attempt to do to keep him tithing. Just one Sunday prior to his pastor's return from Africa, this gentleman stated he was in church and a prophetess approached him and began to say things such as:

"God said you are highly favored and blessed and God want you to know that you are on the right path and that he is going to use you mightily and so forth and so on." The prophetess was the senior pastor's wife. (These things I heard with my own ears, because he recorded the entire prophecy)

Once the senior pastor returned from his trip, he gained the knowledge that this gentleman was no longer a tither; the next Sunday after his wife prophesied to him about how God was with him and etc.; the senior pastor began reprimanding him during the Sunday morning service; telling him that he had been possessed by demons.

Is that what we are coming to now where we are using scare tactics to get people to do what we desire instead of using biblical knowledge from the word of God?

Tithing is not a spiritual act unlike free will giving. Free will giving is strictly a voluntary act that brings about you having to make a decision based on your mind, your will, your intellect and your emotions. Tithing is not free willed; it is similar to the way we pay taxes. It is

Culmination

enforced and regulated by laws with no options to refuse. If you do not pay taxes and get audited, you will be held responsible for not obeying the rules and regulations set forth that governs that particular tax situation. Tithing should be viewed in the same manner – if you are going to punish someone for not tithing; you should not be making it a spiritual situation and telling people that they are possessed with demons. I've never seen in the bible how people can acquire demons based on their neglect of tithing.

How come the pastor couldn't sit with this gentleman on a different day, other than Sunday morning, and show him scripturally where he may be mistaken instead of embarrassing him and his family in front of the entire congregation. However, there is a reason for that type of behavior and it's a two-fold explanation:

1. It's done to persuade people that God continues to recognize and require everyone to pay tithes with an attempt to convince people that those words spoken are coming directly from heaven (as a revelation of some sort).

2. It's done to place fear in the hearts of those who are present and listening; as a warning to those who may be considering this idea of not tithing.

The sad thing is this gentleman was humiliated and chastised in front of the whole church with no consideration for his soul – over a few bucks. See, this is what I don't understand – if a person didn't believe that God is love, someone will take the time to sit with you, show, and teach you biblically that our God is a loving God and petition you to ask questions.

If a person didn't believe that Christ is the Son of God, someone will take the time to sit with you, show, and teach you biblically the existence of Christ and his relationship to God and petition you to ask questions.

But when it comes to tithing, as I was informed by this gentleman, his senior Pastor told him that he doesn't have to prove anything to him, implying "he don't need to understand -- he just have to believe."

Now, how ironic is that?

I remember when my family and I was living in Virginia and we visited this particular church for about two Sundays. During the time we visited this church, the pastor was speaking about the nature of giving and tithing – using a lot of non biblical clichés. So, after the service, my wife approached the pastor about some of the things he was stating during service. The pastor kindly informed my wife to contact him via email and he will be more than happy to answer her questions. So, when we arrived home that day; I got on my computer and sent the pastor a list of questions; attaching the information that I learned about tithing. Days later, he responded to us via email stating, "I see that you are real serious into this subject and I would like to inform you that we as a church do not believe or accept that way of thinking and I graciously ask that you and your family do not come back to this church again. *We were only visitors at the time.*

Tithing is indeed a type of financial bondage. No, not of sin but, yes, oppression. It is like being bound with steel cords, although promised liberty but never seeming to gain or maintain freedom. Tithing reminds me metaphorically of the year 1865, when the civil war ended and the thirteenth amendment was added to the U.S. constitution to abolish slavery. Though slavery was now legally abolished, many were held against their will/forced to remain in slavery because of a lack of education, not having the knowledge/wherewithal to go, to live, and to survive. Their essential needs for survival, or how to survive, still remained unclear. But, as the years progressed and education became readily available, many gained the knowledge to pursue a life of freedom. I truly believe that in 1865 ignorance was the prisoner of their minds, but then education became the freedom to their souls. Christ abolished the custom of tithing because he nailed the law and all its practices to that old rugged cross-which preceded his death.

What is your excuse for remaining in bondage, although that law had been abolished long ago? Will you remain captive due to the ignorance of the law, or will you be educated to freedom? Are you afraid of the mockery from those who oppose your independence? Will you continue to remain in bondage for the rest of your existence for fear of persecution, or will you resist these restrictions, withstand the pressure, and live a life with purpose?

Culmination

I hope and pray that you stand up in Christ and challenge those who impose on your freedom. I know that many who have read this book in its entirety have been confronted with something totally new and out of their normal comfort zone of believing; however, true freedom comes on the execution of the knowledge received. Why read and rejoice about freedom, but still choose to live in bondage? No! Tithing today IS NOT SIN, but it is a type of bondage. No! Not spiritual bondage but, yes, indeed, financial bondage. I believe that you should always be a freewill giver, not manipulated or forced to give. I believe in not making a huge public announcement about the people who give the most in abundance while making those who give less feel less important.

Freewill giving should be a private declaration between you and God and/or your immediate family and God; and, Christ's churches must get back to depending on God by faith to maintain the church's financial burden. If the church needs financial help, they should make an open declaration to its members and encourage them to freely give, and if there is a specific amount that's needed, that amount should be explained in complete detail, along with the true purpose behind the request. Not in exploitation, but in a freewill declaration as the children of Israel did in building the tabernacle of God, which was not required as a law of Moses. Though it was God's building that was being constructed, it was still their free will to make contributions for the needs of the tabernacle.

Remember, in Exodus 35:4, Moses told the nation of Israel that the Lord had commanded for them to build the tabernacle of the Lord. Even though the tabernacle had been commanded to be built, Moses told the people that whoever is of a "willing and generous heart" to give an offering for the service of the Lord. And, because Moses did not force the people to give, the passage of Scriptures states that those who were of a willing heart came and brought an offering, not to be used for the self-gratification and pleasures of Moses, but used for the construction of the tabernacle/tent of meeting for all its service and the holy garments. You will find that the offering throughout the Bible consisted of gold, silver, linens, materials, etc., but you will never find biblically that money (gold or silver) was requested or given as a tithe according to the Law of Moses. It is our duty to become willing vessels to give but no one should be forced or placed in oppression under a previous requirement to do so. If you desire to still believe that we must pay tithes according the law, then you are at liberty to believe, but do understand that you are not paying tithes under the new covenant, because Christ never required this custom. The only people who still require this routine are those you hear every Sunday morning who have not freed you from financial bondage. As it was in the days of this country's history, when many were emancipated from slavery, there were still many that maintained slavery as law. If anyone chooses to live in the lack of knowledge about the practices of tithing that is their choice, but don't allow their choices to become your choices. Choose to follow Christ and live freely in his new covenant.

Introduction

Notes Page

_____

_____

_____

_____

_____

_____

_____

Chapter 1
Tithing Before the Law

Notes Page

_____

_____

_____

_____

_____

_____

_____

Chapter 2
Mosaic Law On Tithing

Notes Page

_____

_____

_____

_____

_____

_____

_____

Chapter 3
The Malachi Prophecy

Notes Page

_____

_____

_____

_____

_____

_____

_____

Chapter 4
The New Testament and Tithing

Notes Page

_____

_____

_____

_____

_____

_____

Chapter 5
The Old vs. The New Covenant

Notes Page

_____

_____

_____

_____

_____

_____

Chapter 6
Culmination

Notes Page

_____

_____

_____

_____

_____

_____

_____

www.ingramcontent.com/pod-product-compliance
Lightning Source LLC
LaVergne TN
LVHW021347080426
835508LV00020B/2153